ROLLING Along

NANCY J. MARTIN

ROLLING Along
Easy Quilts from 2½" Strips

JELLY ROLL FRIENDLY

Martingale®
& COMPANY

CREDITS

President & CEO - Tom Wierzbicki

Publisher - Jane Hamada

Editorial Director - Mary V. Green

Managing Editor - Tina Cook

Developmental Editor - Karen Costello Soltys

Technical Editor - Ellen Pahl

Copy Editor - Liz McGehee

Design Director - Stan Green

Assistant Design Director - Regina Girard

Illustrator - Laurel Strand

Cover & Text Designer - Shelly Garrison

Photographer - Brent Kane

MISSION STATEMENT

Dedicated to providing quality products and service to inspire creativity.

ISBN: 978-1-56477-841-3

ACKNOWLEDGMENTS

Many thanks to the fine quilters who helped me
finish the quilts on time: Shelly Nolte, Wanda
Rains, and Frankie Schmidt. Your quilting skills
are much appreciated.

Thanks to Cleo Nollette, who has perfected the art
of speed sewing to help me make my deadlines.

My overwhelming gratitude to the staff of
Martingale & Company who always make
my books so appealing.

And thanks to my husband, Dan, for
encouragement, computer support,
and shoulder massages.

CONTENTS

INTRODUCTION ⬦⬦⬦⬦⬦⬦⬦⬦⬦⬦⬦⬦⬦⬦⬦⬦⬦⬦⬦⬦⬦

Want to make a quilt in a jiffy? Using precut color-coordinated strips

can help speed up your project. There is no need to spend time selecting fabrics, cutting strips,

and then returning all of that unused fabric to your stash. Just unroll or open the package of strips

and you're ready to go.

Several of the quilts in this book use only 2½" strips, while others combine the strips with

additional scraps of fabric. Using this approach, you will have fabric to use as background material

in appliqué quilts, as in "Posy Pots" on page 38, or the ability to integrate half-square triangles into

quilt designs, as in "Barn Raising" shown on the opposite page.

Packages of 2½"-wide precut fabric strips in various color schemes are available from several

manufacturers. Jelly Rolls are Moda's new fabric product, a package of forty 2½"-wide strips rolled

into a bundle that resembles a jelly roll. They are very visually appealing and hard to resist.

Moda's Jelly Rolls come in several different fabric lines, ranging from traditional to contemporary.

Look for these fabric rolls or other prepackaged bundles of strips in your local quilt shop or online.

None of the quilts in this book are fabric-specific. In other words, you could make any of the

quilts using any collection of strips. I just chose the fabric combinations

that appealed to me. Feel free to do the same, and don't

hesitate to cut a few strips from your stash to go with a

strip collection that you have purchased.

QUILTS from Strips

Strip, or "string," quilts emerged early in the history of quiltmaking. Because commercial bedding was not readily available until about 1860, most bed coverings were fashioned at home. These were not "best" quilts. They were necessary for warmth, and were referred to as utility quilts or strip quilts. These strip quilts featured myriad fabrics from leftover clothing, linens, and bedding, and they were not necessarily color coordinated.

My strip quilts are carefully planned for color and placement; thus they aren't random strip quilts in the historical sense of the term. I use a technique that I refer to as a color recipe to plan the fabric placement in my quilts. This technique helps to simplify color selection. Think in terms of color groups rather than individual colors when using a color recipe. Having chosen a

tentative color recipe based on your color preference, select a range of fabrics for each color group in the recipe. If blue is one of the colors, use several blue prints in differing intensities and visual texture. Using the packages of precut 2½"-wide strips gives you the variety of fabric that you need to make a stunning strip quilt.

Background fabrics are particularly important in creating variations in the contrast of the blocks. For a scrappy background, the range can extend from bright whites to ecru and more medium tones. The whites will add sparkle to the quilt and lead the eye from one part of the quilt to the next. Or you may choose to use just one fabric for the background, as I did for "Posy Pots" shown below, to showcase the bright colors of the strips.

TOOLS of the Trade ◇◇◇◇◇◇◇◇◇◇◇◇◇◇◇◇◇◇◇◇◇◇◇◇◇◇◇◇

Quiltmaking, whether you're using strips or not, requires some basic tools. The following is a list of items I use each time I make a project.

Sewing machine: Stitching quilts on a sewing machine is easy and enjoyable. Spend some time getting to know your machine and become comfortable with its use. Keep your machine dust free and well oiled.

Machine piecing does not require an elaborate sewing machine. All you need is a straight-stitch machine in good working order. It should make an evenly locked straight stitch that looks the same on both the top and bottom of the seam. Adjust the tension, if needed, to produce smooth, evenly stitched seams.

Pins: A good supply of glass- or plastic-headed pins is necessary. Long pins are especially helpful when pinning thick layers together. If you plan to machine quilt, you will need to hold the layers of the quilt together with a large supply of rustproof, size 2 safety pins.

Iron and ironing board: Frequent and careful pressing is necessary to ensure smooth, accurately stitched blocks and quilt tops. Place your iron and ironing board, along with a plastic spray bottle of water, close to your sewing machine.

Needles: Use sewing-machine needles sized for cotton fabrics (size 70/10 or 80/12). You also need hand-sewing needles (Sharps) and hand-quilting needles (Betweens in sizes 8, 9, and 10).

Scissors: Use good-quality shears, and use them only for cutting fabric. Thread snips or embroidery scissors are handy for clipping stray threads.

Seam ripper: This little tool will come in handy if you find it necessary to remove a seam before resewing.

Rotary cutter and mat: A large rotary cutter enables you to quickly cut strips and pieces without templates. A cutting mat is essential to protect both the blade and the table on which you're cutting. An 18" x 24" mat allows you to cut long strips on the straight or bias grain. You might also consider purchasing a smaller mat to use when working with scraps.

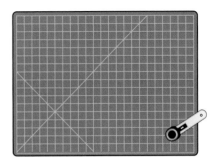

Rotary-cutting rulers: Use a see-through ruler to measure fabric and guide the rotary cutter. There are many appropriate rulers on the market. Make sure the one you choose includes markings for 45° and 60° angles and guidelines for cutting strips in standard size measurements. Select a ruler that is marked with large, clear numbers and does not have a lot of confusing lines.

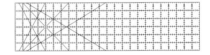

The Bias Square® ruler is critical for cutting accurate bias squares. This acrylic ruler is available in three sizes—4", 6", or 8" square—and is ruled with 1/8" markings. It features a diagonal line, which is placed on the bias seam, enabling you to cut an accurately sewn square that looks exactly like one sewn using two triangles.

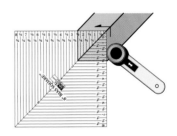

QUILTMAKING Basics ✕✕✕✕✕✕✕✕✕✕✕✕✕✕✕✕✕✕✕✕

In this section, you'll find instructions for the techniques used throughout the book to make the quilt tops and for finishing your quilts.

CUTTING STRIPS

If you haven't purchased a package or bundle of precut strips, use the following directions to cut strips from your fabric stash. Adding additional fabrics can also provide an accent color or a greater variation of colors in the quilt.

1. Cut all strips on the crosswise grain of fabric.

2. Fold and press the fabric with selvages matching, aligning the crosswise grains as much as possible. If the fabric is badly off-grain, pull diagonally to straighten as shown. It is impossible to rotary-cut fabrics exactly on the straight grain of fabric since many fabrics are printed off-grain. In rotary cutting, straight, even cuts are made as close to the grain as possible. A slight variation will not affect your project.

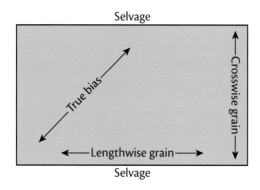

3. Place the folded fabric on the rotary-cutting mat, with the folded edge closest to your body. Align the Bias Square ruler with the fold of the fabric and place a longer cutting ruler to the left as shown.

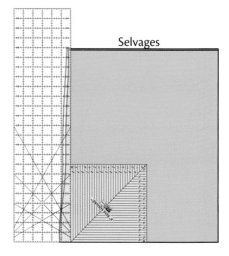

4. Remove the Bias Square ruler and make a cut along the right side of the longer ruler to square up the edge of the fabric. Hold the ruler in place with your left hand, placing your little finger off the edge of the ruler to serve as an anchor and prevent slipping.

5. Align the 2½" measurement on the ruler with the newly cut edge of the fabric to cut 2½" strips for the quilts in this book.

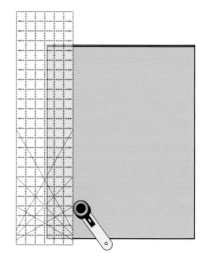

SEWING STRIPS

Strip piecing eliminates the long and tedious repetition of sewing small individual pieces together; however, it usually produces identical units. I prefer that each strip-pieced unit contains a variety of fabrics; each time that I sew strips into a strip set, I select a different combination of strips.

Most of the units for the quilts in this book are sewn from 2½" x 22" strips. The exception is "Sunny Days" (page 32), where individual pieces are cut before sewing. If you have strips that have been cut selvage to selvage along the crosswise grain, just cut them in half on the fold. This works well for a number of reasons.

- It helps keep fabrics on-grain and eliminates the bowing or curving that may occur when fabrics of differing thread counts are used.

- You can get more fabric variation in your quilt design if there are fewer identical strip sets.

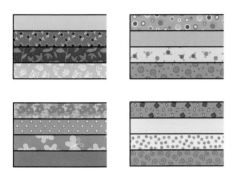

- If you purchase fat quarters to add variety to your strips, it will be easy to cut these 2½" x 22" strips.
- Some purchased bundles of strips repeat the same fabric design in varying colors. Using the shorter strips can keep the same design from repeating within a strip set.

The most important skill in strip piecing is sewing an accurate ¼"-wide seam. You can purchase a special ¼" foot that is sized so you can align the edge of your fabric with the edge of the presser foot, resulting in a seam that is exactly ¼" from the fabric edge. You can also mark a guide on your sewing machine using painter's tape or masking tape.

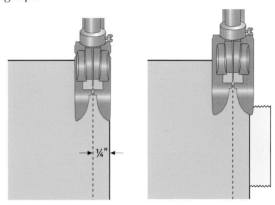

Accurate Strip Sets

Each project that uses the strip-piecing technique will indicate the number of strips needed from each color of fabric. If you need to add more strips, make sure they are cut on the crosswise grain.

1. Refer to the project instructions to sew the strips together along the long edges. Press the seams toward the darker fabric, pressing from the right side so the fabric won't pleat along the seam lines.

2. Straighten the right end of each strip set by aligning a horizontal line of the cutting ruler with one of the strip set's internal seams. Cut along the right edge of the ruler. Place the straightened end on the left, align the desired measurement on your cutting ruler with the straightened end, and cut.

BASIC BIAS-SQUARE TECHNIQUE

Many traditional quilt patterns contain squares made from two contrasting half-square triangles. The short sides of the triangles are on the straight grain of fabric while the long sides are on the bias. These are called bias-square units. Using a bias strip-piecing method, you can easily sew and cut several bias squares at a time. This technique is especially useful for small bias squares, for which pressing after stitching usually distorts the shape (and sometimes results in burned fingers). Follow the steps below to make bias squares.

Note: All instructions in this book give the cut size for bias squares; the finished size after stitching will be ½" smaller.

1. Start with two squares of fabric. The project instructions in this book call for a pair of 8" squares. Layer the squares right sides up and cut in half diagonally.

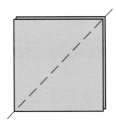

2. Cut the squares into strips, measuring from the previous cut. For the quilts in this book, all strips are cut 2½" wide.

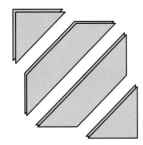

3. Stitch the strips together using ¼"-wide seams to make two pieced units. Be sure to align the strips so the lower edge and one adjacent edge form straight lines.

4. Starting at the lower-left corner, align the 45° mark of the Bias Square ruler on the seam line. Be sure that the lower corner of the fabric extends beyond the

size of the square you need. You want to cut slightly oversize at first. Cut along the side and the top edge to remove the bias square from the rest of the fabric.

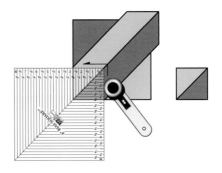

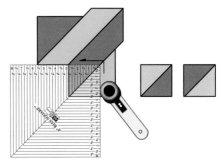

Align 45° mark on seam line
and cut first 2 sides.

5. The next cut is made along the remaining two sides to align the diagonal and trim the bias square to the correct size. To make the cut, rotate the cut unit and place the Bias Square on top. Align the required measurements on both cut sides and align the 45° mark on the seam. Cut the remaining two sides of the bias squares.

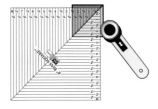

Turn cut segments and
cut opposite 2 sides.

6. Continue cutting bias squares from the bias-strip unit in this manner, working from left to right and from bottom to top, row by row, until you have cut bias squares from all usable fabric. Use the chart on the next page to determine strip width and the number of bias squares you can expect to cut from two squares of fabric.

YIELD OF BIAS SQUARES				
Finished Size	**Cut Size**	**Fabric Size**	**Strip Width**	**Yield**
2"	2½" x 2½"	8" x 8"*	2½"	8
2"	2½" x 2½"	9" x 9"	2½"	14
2⅛"	2⅝" x 2⅝"	8" x 8"	2½"	8
2½"	3" x 3"	8" x 8"	2¾"	8
2½"	3" x 3"	9" x 9"	2¾"	8
3"	3½" x 3½"	9" x 9"	3"	8
A pair of 7" x 7" squares will yield the same number of bias squares.				

MACHINE PIECING

The most important skill in machine piecing is sewing an accurate ¼"-wide seam. This is necessary for seams to match and for the resulting block or quilt to measure the required size. There are several methods that will help you achieve this.

- Purchase a special foot that is sized so that you can align the fabric edge with the edge of the presser foot, resulting in a seam that is ¼" from the fabric edge. Bernina has a special patchwork foot (#37), and Little Foot makes several special ¼" feet that fit most machines.

- If you have an electronic or computerized sewing machine, adjust the needle position so that the resulting seam is ¼" from the fabric edge.

- Find the ¼" seam allowance on your machine by placing an accurate template under the presser foot and lowering the needle onto the seam line; mark the seam allowance by placing a piece of masking tape at the edge of the template. You can use several layers of masking tape, building up a raised edge to guide your fabric. You can also use a piece of moleskin for a raised seam guide.

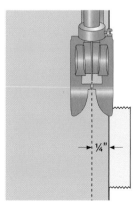

Test to make sure that the method you're using results in an accurate ¼"-wide seam.

1. Cut three strips of fabric, 1½" x 3".

2. Sew the strips together, using the edge of the presser foot or the seam guide you have made.

3. Press seams toward the outer edges. After sewing and pressing, the center strip should measure exactly 1" wide. If it doesn't, adjust the needle or seam guide in the proper direction.

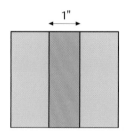

Matching Seams

When sewing the fabric pieces that make up a unit or block, follow the piecing diagrams provided. Press each group of pieces before joining it to the next unit, referring to the arrows in the diagrams for pressing direction.

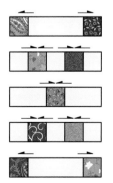

Stitch and then press.

Join the units.

There are several techniques you can use to get your seams to match perfectly.

Opposing seams: When stitching one seamed unit to another, press seams that need to match in opposite directions. The two "opposing" seams will hold each other in place and evenly distribute the fabric bulk. Plan pressing to take advantage of opposing seams.

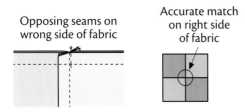

Opposing seams on wrong side of fabric

Accurate match on right side of fabric

Positioning pin: A pin, carefully pushed straight through two points that need to match, will establish the proper matching point. Pin the remainder of the seam normally and remove the positioning pin just before stitching.

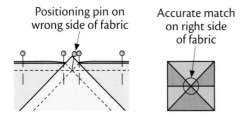

Positioning pin on wrong side of fabric

Accurate match on right side of fabric

The X: When triangles are pieced, the stitches will form an X at the next seam line. Stitch through the center of the X to make sure the points on the sewn triangles will not be cut off.

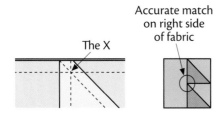

Accurate match on right side of fabric

The X

PRECISE PIECING

A good habit to develop is to use a seam ripper or long pin to gently guide the fabric up to the needle. You can hold seam intersections together or make minor adjustments before the fabric is sewn.

Easing: When two pieces you're sewing together are supposed to match but are slightly different in length, pin the points to match and stitch with the shorter piece on top. The feed dogs will ease in the fullness of the bottom piece.

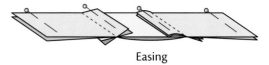

Easing

Inspect each intersection from the right side to see that it's matched. If the seams don't meet accurately, note which direction you need to move the fabric. Use a seam ripper to rip out the seam intersection and ½" of stitching on either side of the intersection. Shift fabric to correct the alignment, place positioning pins, and then restitch.

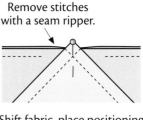

Remove stitches with a seam ripper.

Shift fabric, place positioning pin, and restitch.

Pressing: After stitching a seam, it's important to press your work. Careful pressing helps make the next steps in the stitching process, such as matching points or aligning seams, easier. Follow the direction of the arrows in the diagrams when pressing seams to one side.

When stitching quilt blocks together, you may find that previously pressed seams do not align as opposing seams. To correct this, I pin one of the seams in the other direction to create opposing seams. After stitching the seam, I press the seam allowance in its new direction using a steam iron and working gently.

Be sure to press, not iron, your work. Ironing is an aggressive back-and-forth motion that we use on clothing to remove wrinkles. This action can pull and stretch the bias edges or seams in your piecing. Perfectly marked and sewn quilt pieces can easily be distorted by excessive ironing. Pressing is the gentle lowering, pressing, and lifting of the iron along the length of the fabric without moving the iron back and forth along the seam. Let the heat, steam, and an occasional spritz of water press the fabric in the desired direction.

Chain Piecing

Chain piecing is an assembly-line approach to stitching your blocks together. Rather than sewing each block from start to finish, you can sew identical units of each block together at one time, streamlining the process. It's a good idea, however, to sew one sample block together from start to finish to ensure that the pieces have been accurately cut and that you have the proper positioning and coloration for each piece.

Stack the units you will be sewing in pairs, arranging any opposing seam allowances so that the top seam allowance faces toward the needle and the lower seam allowance faces toward you. Then you won't need to keep checking to see if the lower seam is being pulled to the wrong side by the feed dogs as you feed the fabric through the sewing machine.

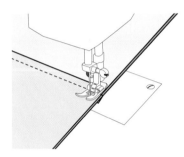

Face top seam allowance toward
the needle whenever possible.

Feed units through the machine without stopping to cut thread. There will be a "stitch" or small length of thread between the units.

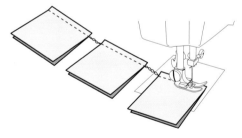

Take the connected units to the ironing board for pressing and then clip them apart. Chain piecing takes a little planning, but it saves you time and thread.

Use a "thread saver" to begin and end all your seams. Keep a stack of fabric scraps, about 2" x 2", near your machine. When you begin to sew, fold one of the squares in half and sew to its edge. Leave the presser foot down and continue sewing onto your piecing unit. When you have finished sewing a seam or chain piecing, sew onto another thread saver, leaving the needle in place and the presser foot down. This thread saver will be in place for sewing the next seam or unit.

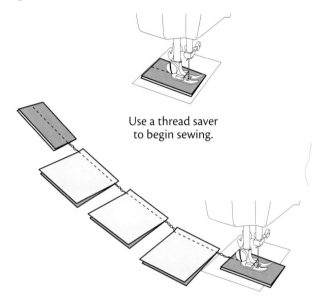

Use a thread saver
to begin sewing.

End sewing with
a thread saver.

This technique saves thread because you don't stop and pull a length of thread to remove fabric from the machine. All the tails of thread will be on the thread saver and not on the back of the block or quilt. This method also keeps the machine from pulling or distorting the edges of the fabric as you start a seam.

APPLIQUÉ

Some of the quilts in this book have appliquéd accents. You can use the paper-patch technique for all the pieces except stems. For stems, use the bias-stem method.

Paper-Patch Appliqué

1. Make a template of each shape in the appliqué design using template plastic or other stiff material. Don't add seam allowances to the templates.

2. On bond-weight paper or freezer paper, trace around the templates to make a paper patch for each shape in the appliqué.

3. Pin each paper patch to the wrong side of the fabric. If using freezer paper, pin with the plastic-coated side face up.

4. Cut out the fabric shapes, adding a ⅛"-wide seam allowance around each paper shape.

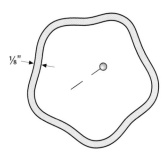

⅛"

5. With your fingers, turn the seam allowance over the edge of the paper and baste to the paper. Clip corners and baste inside curves first. (A little clipping may be necessary to help the fabric stretch.) On outside curves, take small running stitches through the fabric only, to ease in fullness.

6. For sharply pointed corners, such as the leaves in "Posy Pots" and "Holly Stars," first fold the corner to the inside; then fold the remaining seam allowances over the paper.

Fold corners to inside.

Fold remaining seam allowances over paper.

BASTING HINT

Take an occasional stitch through the paper to hold the fabric in place.

7. When all the seam allowances are turned and basted, press the appliqué pieces.

Bias Stems

Bias stems are easy to make with the help of metal or nylon bias press bars, also known as Celtic bars. These handy notions are available at most quilt shops. The following steps describe the process of making bias stems with bias bars.

1. Cut the fabric for the stems into bias strips the width indicated in the instructions.

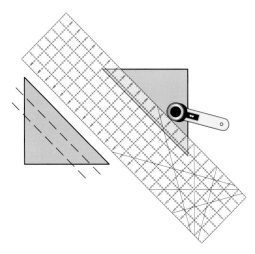

2. Fold each bias strip in half, wrong sides together, and stitch ⅛" from the long raw edges to form a tube.

Stitch ⅛" from edges.

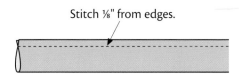

3. Insert the appropriate size of bias bar into the tube, roll the seam to the underside, and press flat. Remove the bias bar.

Bias bar

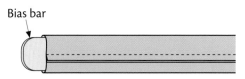

4. Cut the bias tube to the lengths needed and place them on the background fabric, forming the desired shape. Pin (or baste) and appliqué the pieces in place.

STITCHING THE APPLIQUÉS

1. Fold the background fabric in quarters (some placement guides indicate diagonal folds) and lightly crease.

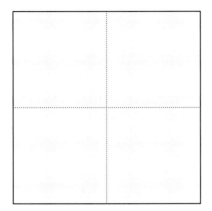

2. Position and pin the pieces in place on the background fabric, following the numbered order.

3. Copy the placement guide onto tracing paper or a transparent sheet and place it over the pinned appliqué pieces to check for accuracy. Make any necessary corrections.

Transparency sheet

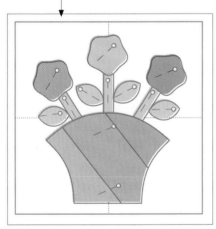

4. Follow the numbers on the placement guide when appliquéing the fabric piece to the block, easing fullness and bias stretch outward.

Wrong side of background

5. Use a small blind hem stitch and a single strand of thread that matches the appliqué (for example, pink thread for a pink flower) to appliqué shapes to the background fabric.

6. Start the first stitch from the back of the block. Bring the needle up through the background fabric and through the folded edge of the appliqué piece.

7. Insert the needle right next to where you brought it up, but this time put it through only the background fabric.

8. Bring the needle up through the background fabric and then into the appliqué piece, approximately 1/8" or less from the first stitch.

9. Space your stitches a little less than 1/8" apart.

10. When the appliqué is complete, slit the background fabric behind the appliqué shape and pull out the paper patch. For bias stems, there is no need to cut the background fabric.

FINISHING techniques

This section includes tips for completing a quilt with confidence and pride. These techniques work well for me, but they are by no means the only methods for finishing your quilt. If a technique is new to you, try it; you might find that you incorporate the technique into your quilt-making process from now on.

ADDING BORDERS

Borders can be used to frame and soften a busy design. They are also helpful in enlarging a quilt to fit a standard-size bed. It isn't always necessary to have a border on a quilt, however. Many antique quilts made from scraps have no borders, since continuous yardage was scarce and expensive.

Straighten the edges of your quilt top before adding borders. There should be little or no trimming needed for a straight-set quilt.

To find the correct measurement for straight-cut border strips, always measure through the center of the quilt, not at the outside edges. This ensures that the borders are of equal length on opposite sides of the quilt and brings the outer edges in line with the center dimension if discrepancies exist. Otherwise, your quilt might not be "square" due to minor piecing variations and/or stretching that occurred while you worked with the blocks. If there is a large size difference between the two sides, it is better to go back and correct the source of the problem rather than try to make the border fit and end up with a distorted quilt.

The easiest border to add is a border with butted corners. This method has been used on all the quilts with borders in this book. You will save fabric if you attach the border strips to the longest sides first and then to the remaining two sides.

1. Measure the length of the quilt through the center. Cut two border strips to this measurement.

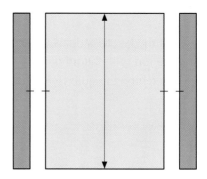

Measure center of quilt,
top to bottom.

Border strips cut on the crosswise grain will need to be pieced together first and then cut to the exact size. Border strips cut on the lengthwise grain are cut longer than necessary to allow for any variances in the quilt-top size. Cut them to the exact size before adding to the quilt top.

SMART SEAMS

When joining border strips, the seam will be less noticeable and stronger if it is pieced on an angle.

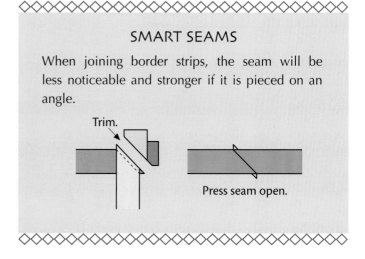

2. Mark the centers of the border strips and the quilt top. Pin the borders to the sides of the quilt, matching centers and ends and easing or slightly stretching the quilt to fit the border strip as necessary.

3. Sew the side borders in place and press the seams toward the borders.

4. Measure the width of the quilt through the center, including the side borders, to determine the length of the top and bottom borders. Cut the border strips to this measurement, piecing strips as necessary. Mark the centers of the border strips and the quilt top. Pin borders to the top and bottom of the quilt top, easing or slightly stretching the quilt to fit as necessary.

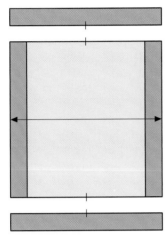

Measure center of quilt,
side to side, including borders.
Mark centers.

5. Sew the top and bottom borders in place and press the seams toward the borders.

MARKING THE QUILTING DESIGN

Whether you machine or hand quilt, you may need to mark a quilting design on the quilt top before layering and basting. If you will be stitching in the ditch, outlining the design ¼" away from all seams, stitching a grid of straight lines using masking tape as a guide, or stitching a meandering, free-motion design, you do not need to mark the design.

• To stitch in the ditch, place the stitches in the valley created next to the seam. Stitch on the side that does not have the seam allowance under it.

Quilting in the ditch

• To outline a design, stitch ¼" from the seam inside each shape.

Outline quilting

• To mark a grid or pattern of lines, use ¼"-wide masking tape in 15" to 18" lengths. Place strips of tape on a small area and quilt next to the edge of the tape. Remove the tape when stitching is complete. You can reuse the tape to mark another area. *Caution:* Don't leave tape on a quilt top for an extended length of time because it may leave a sticky residue.

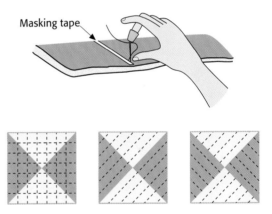

Masking tape

• To mark complex or repeated designs, use a stencil. Quilting stencils made from durable plastic are available in quilt shops. There is a groove cut into the plastic, wide enough to allow the use of a marking device. Just place the marker inside the groove to quickly transfer the design to the fabric. Good removable marking pencils include Berol silver pencils, EZ Washout marking pencils, mechanical pencils, and sharp regular pencils. Just be sure to draw lines lightly, and always test your marker on a scrap of fabric for removability.

• Use a light table to trace more intricate designs from books or drawn patterns.

To make your own light table:

Separate your dining-room table as if you're adding an extra leaf. Then place a piece of glass, plastic, or Plexiglas over the opening. (I use the removable glass from a storm door for safety's sake, because there is a frame around the edge of the glass.) Have the glass (or glass substitute) cut to fit your table at a glass shop, if desired, and frame or tape the edges to avoid cut fingers. For an additional fee, you can have glass edges finished to eliminate the sharp edges.

Once the glass is in place, position a table lamp on the floor beneath it to create an instant light table. If your table does not separate, two card tables or end tables of the same height can be pushed together to create a support for the glass.

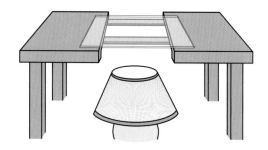

BACKING

For most quilts larger than crib size, you will need to piece the backing from two or more lengths of fabric if you use 42"-wide fabric. Seams can run horizontally or vertically in a pieced backing, as long as the fabric isn't a directional print. Avoid the temptation to use a bed sheet for a backing, since it is difficult to quilt through. Cut backing 3" to 4" larger than the quilt top all around. Be sure to trim away the selvages where pieces are joined.

Plan to put a sleeve or rod pocket on the back of the quilt if you want to hang it. (See "Adding a Quilt Sleeve" on page 27.) You may want to purchase extra backing fabric so that the sleeve and the backing match.

BATTING

There are many types of batting to choose from. Select a high-loft batting for a bed quilt that you want to look puffy. Lightweight battings are fine for baby quilts or wall hangings. A lightweight batting is easier to quilt through and shows the quilting design well. It also gives your quilt an antique, old-fashioned look.

Polyester batting works well, doesn't shift after washing, and is easy to quilt through. It comes in lightweight and regular lofts as well as in fat, or high-loft, batting for comforters.

Cotton batting is a good choice if you're quilting an old quilt top or if you want to achieve the look of a vintage quilt. Some cotton battings must be quilted with stitches no more than 2" apart, but check the packaging for this information.

COORDINATE YOUR BATTING

Dark batting works well behind a dark quilt top. If there is any bearding (batting fibers creeping through the top), it will not be as noticeable.

LAYERING AND BASTING

Open a package of batting and smooth it out flat. Allow the batting to rest in this position for at least 24 hours. Press the backing so that all seams are flat and the fold lines have been removed.

A large dining-room table, Ping-Pong table, or two large folding tables pushed together make an ideal work surface on which to prepare your quilt. Use a table pad to protect your dining-room table. The floor is not a good choice for layering your quilt. It requires you to do too much bending, and the layers can easily shift or be disturbed.

Place the backing on the table with the wrong side of the fabric facing up. If the table is large enough, you may want to tape the backing down with masking tape. Spread your batting over the backing, centering it, and smooth out any remaining folds.

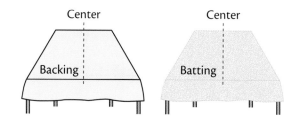

Center the freshly pressed and marked quilt top on these two layers. Check all four sides to make sure there is adequate batting and backing. Stretch the backing to make sure it is still smooth.

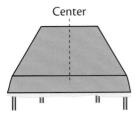

Center

The basting method you use depends on whether you will quilt by hand or machine. Use thread basting for hand quilting, or safety-pin basting for machine quilting.

Thread Basting

Starting in the center of the quilt top, baste the three layers together with straight pins while gently smoothing out the fullness to the sides and corners. Take care not to distort the borders and any straight lines within the quilt design.

After pinning, baste the layers together with a needle and light-colored thread, so the thread color won't bleed onto the quilt. Start in the middle and make a line of long stitches to each corner to form a large X.

Continue basting in a grid of parallel lines 6" to 8" apart. Finish with a row of basting around the outside edges. Quilts that you quilt with a hoop or on your lap will be handled more than those quilted on a frame; therefore, they require more basting. After basting, remove the pins. Now you're ready to quilt.

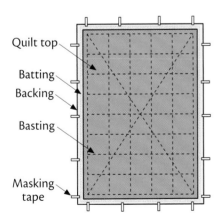

Quilt top
Batting
Backing
Basting
Masking tape

Pin Basting

A quick way to baste a quilt top is with size 2 safety pins. They are large enough to catch all three layers but not so large that they snag fine fabric. Begin pinning in the center and work out toward the edges. Place pins 4" to 5" apart.

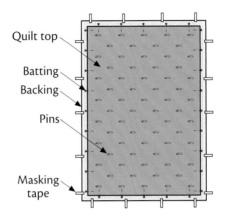

Quilt top
Batting
Backing
Pins
Masking tape

Use long, straight pins along the outside edge to hold everything in place. Place pins perpendicular to the edge, 1½" to 2" apart. Remove the pins after basting is complete.

HAND QUILTING

To quilt by hand, you need quilting thread, quilting needles (called Betweens), small scissors, a thimble, and perhaps a balloon or large rubber band to help grasp the needle if it gets stuck. Quilt with a freestanding frame or with a large hoop on your lap. Use a single strand of quilting thread no longer than 18". Make a small, single knot at the end of the thread. The quilting stitch is a small running stitch that goes through all three layers of the quilt. Take two, three, or even four stitches at a time if you can keep them even. When crossing seams, you might find it necessary to "hunt and peck" or "stab" one stitch at a time.

To begin, insert the needle in the top layer about 1" from the point where you want to start stitching. Pull the needle out at the desired starting point and gently tug at the knot until it pops through the fabric and is buried in the batting. Make a backstitch and begin quilting. Stitches should be tiny (8 to 10 per inch is good), even, and straight; tiny stitches will come with practice.

When you almost reach the end of the thread, make a single knot ¼" from the fabric. Take a backstitch to bury the knot in the batting. Run the thread off through the batting and out the quilt top; then snip it off. The first and last stitches will look different from the running stitches in between. To make them less noticeable, start and stop where quilting lines cross each other or at seam joins. Remove the basting thread when the quilting is finished.

Hand-quilting stitch

MACHINE QUILTING

Machine quilting is a good choice for finishing quilt tops in less time. It's also a practical choice for baby quilts or other items that will need lots of washing.

Machine quilting on a home sewing machine works best for small projects and beginners; it can be difficult to feed the bulk of a large quilt through a sewing machine.

Use a walking foot or even-feed foot (or the built-in even-feed feature, when available) for your sewing machine to help the quilt layers feed through the machine without shifting or puckering. This type of foot is essential for straight-line and grid quilting and for large, simple curves. Read your machine's instruction manual for special tension settings to sew through the extra layer of batting.

Walking foot

Curved designs require free fabric movement under the foot of the sewing machine. This is called free-motion quilting, and with a little practice, you can imitate beautiful hand-quilting designs quickly. If you wish to quilt curved designs with your machine, use a darning foot and lower the feed dogs. Because the feed dogs are lowered for free-motion quilting, the speed at which you run the machine and feed the fabric under the foot determines the stitch length. Practice running the machine fairly fast, which makes it easier to sew smooth lines of quilting.

With free-motion quilting, guide the fabric as if the needle were a stationary pencil drawing the lines of your design.

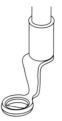

Darning foot

Practice first on a piece of fabric until you get the feel of controlling the motion of the fabric with your hands. Stitch some free-form scribbles, zigzags, and curves. Try a heart or a star. Then practice on a sample block with batting and backing. Make sure your chair is adjusted to a comfortable height. This type of quilting may feel awkward at first, but with a little determination and practice you'll be able to complete a project with beautiful machine quilting in just a few hours.

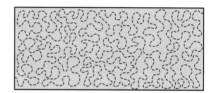

Free-motion meandering pattern

Keep the spacing between quilting lines consistent over the entire quilt. Avoid using complex, little designs and leaving large unquilted spaces. For most battings, a 2" or 3" square is the largest area that can be left unquilted. Read the instructions enclosed with the batting you've chosen.

When all the quilting has been completed, remove the safety pins. Sometimes it is necessary to remove safety pins as you work.

PACE YOURSELF

Don't try to machine quilt an entire quilt in one sitting, even if it's a small project. Break the work into short periods, and stretch and relax your muscles regularly.

BINDING THE EDGES

My favorite quilt binding is a double-layer French binding made from bias strips. It rolls over the edges of the quilt nicely, and the two layers of fabric resist wear. If you use 2¼"-wide strips, the finished width of this binding will be ³⁄₈".

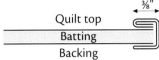

Quilt top
Batting
Backing

Double-layer French binding

The quilt instructions tell you how much fabric to purchase for binding. If, however, you enlarge your quilt or need to compute binding fabric, use the following handy chart. Determine the distance around your quilt and add about 10" for turning the corners and for overlapping the ends of the binding strips.

YARDAGE FOR BIAS BINDING	
Length of Binding	**Fabric Needed**
115"	¼ yard*
180"	³⁄₈ yard*
255"	½ yard
320"	⁵⁄₈ yard
400"	¾ yard
465"	⁷⁄₈ yard

It's a good idea to purchase ½ yard of fabric so the bias strips will be longer and the binding won't have as many seams.

After quilting, trim excess batting and backing even with the edges of the quilt top. A rotary cutter and long ruler will ensure accurate straight edges. If the basting is no longer in place, baste all three layers together at the outer edges. If you intend to attach a sleeve or rod pocket, make one now to attach with the binding. See "Adding a Quilt Sleeve" on page 27 for instructions.

To cut bias strips and bind your quilt, follow these steps:

1. Align the 45° marking of a Bias Square along the selvage and place a long ruler's edge against it. Make the first cut.

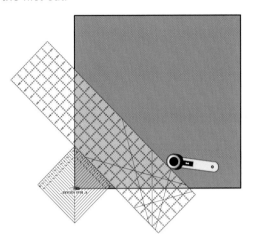

2. Measure the desired width of the strip (2¼") from the cut edge of the fabric. Cut along the edge of the ruler. Continue cutting until you have the number of strips necessary to achieve the required binding length.

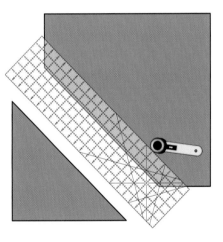

Sometimes a 24"-long ruler may be too short for some of the cuts. After making several cuts, carefully fold the fabric over itself so that the bias edges are even. Continue to cut the bias strips.

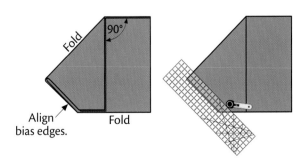

Fold   90°
Align bias edges.   Fold

3. Stitch the bias strips together, offsetting them as shown, to make one continuous strip. Press the seams open.

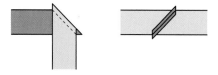

4. Press the strip in half lengthwise, wrong sides together.

5. Unfold the binding at one end and turn under ¼" at a 45° angle as shown.

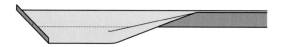

6. Beginning on one side of the quilt, stitch the binding to the quilt, using a ¼"-wide seam allowance. Start stitching 1" to 2" from the start of the binding. Stop stitching ¼" from the corner and backstitch.

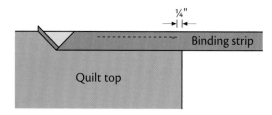

7. Turn the quilt to prepare for sewing along the next edge. Fold the binding away from the quilt at a 45° angle as shown, and then fold again to place the binding along the second edge of the quilt. (This fold creates an angled pleat or miter at the corner.)

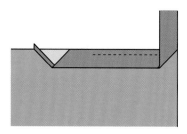

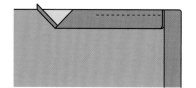

8. Stitch from the fold of the binding along the second edge of the quilt top, stopping ¼" from the corner as you did for the first corner; backstitch. Repeat the stitching and mitering process on the remaining edges and corners of the quilt.

9. When you reach the beginning of the binding, cut the end 1" longer than needed and tuck the end inside the beginning. Stitch the rest of the binding.

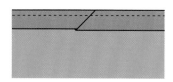

10. Turn the binding to the back of the quilt, over the raw edges, and blindstitch in place so that the folded edge covers the row of machine stitching. At each corner, fold the binding as shown to form a miter on the back of the quilt.

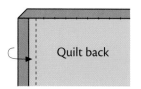

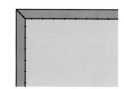

ATTACHING A LABEL

It's a good idea to label a quilt with its name, the name and address of the maker, and the date it was made. Include the name of the quilter(s) if the quilt was quilted by someone other than the maker. On an antique quilt, record all the information you know about the quilt, including where you purchased it. If the quilt is being presented to someone as a gift, also include the recipient's name and the occasion.

To easily make a label, use a permanent-ink pen to print or legibly write all this information on a piece of muslin. Press freezer paper to the back of the muslin to stabilize it while you write. Press raw edges to the wrong side of the label. Remove the freezer paper and stitch the label securely to a lower corner on the back of the quilt. You can also create labels using cross-stitch or embroidery.

FINISHING TECHNIQUES

ADDING A QUILT SLEEVE

If you plan to hang your quilt, attach a sleeve or rod pocket to the back before adding the binding. From leftover backing or other fabric, cut an 8"-wide strip of fabric equal to the width of your quilt. You may need to piece two or three strips together for larger quilts. On each end, fold over ½" and then fold ½" again. Press and stitch by machine.

Fold the strip in half lengthwise, wrong sides together; baste the raw edges to the top edge of the quilt backing. These will be secured when you sew on the binding. Your quilt should be about 1" wider than the sleeve on both sides. Make a little pleat in the sleeve to accommodate the thickness of the rod, and then slipstitch the ends and bottom edge of the sleeve to the backing fabric. This keeps the rod from being inserted next to the quilt backing.

½"   ½"

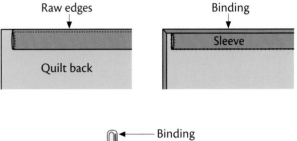

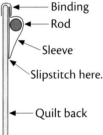

ONE LAST WORD

Now that you are ready to start stitching, stop and think how you can make this quilt uniquely yours. The fabrics that I chose for these quilts are my color preferences and are not the only choices that will work in these quilts. My fabric stash tends to contain many pastels and floral prints, which makes some of these projects soft and feminine looking. However, these very same designs would work in a darker, more muted palette. The choice is yours.

If you feel that your roll or packet of strips doesn't have enough contrast or variety, don't hesitate to cut some strips from your stash. You can add more strips in the same color range or add a splash of an accent color.

Although these quilts do stitch up in a jiffy, they still require careful sewing. The most important skill is sewing an accurate ¼" seam, so do check your seam allowances as you are stitching. Don't hesitate to use some reverse stitching when seams don't line up exactly. You'll be glad that you took the time to pick out a mis-sewn seam and stitch it correctly. Once you get the hang of stitching an accurate ¼" seam, you'll be on a roll. . . .

By Nancy J. Martin, Kingston, Washington, 2006.
Quilted by Wanda Rains, Kingston, Washington.

MAGIC Carpet

Magic Carpet, also known as Many

Trips around the World, is the perfect pattern choice for

these romantic pastel fabrics. Divide your strips into six

color groups and quickly piece together the segments. If

you don't have six different colors of strips, repeat one

color twice, as I did with the white print. You may want to

make the coordinating boudoir pillow found on page 71.

(Be sure to purchase extra fabric if you do.)

Finished Size: 62" x 86" — Block Size: 12" x 12"

MATERIALS

36 strips, 2½" x 22", of white print

18 strips, 2½" x 22", *each* of pink, light green, lavender, and yellow prints

1⅝ yards of yellow floral print for outer border

⅜ yard of lavender print for inner border

5¼ yards of fabric for backing

⅝ yard of fabric for bias binding

70" x 94" piece of batting

CUTTING

From the yellow floral print, cut:
8 strips, 6¼" x 42"

From the lavender print for inner border, cut:
7 strips, 1½" x 42"

MAKING THE BLOCKS

1. Using the 2½" x 22" strips and following the illustrations below, sew three strip sets in each color arrangement to make the units. Press in the direction of the arrows in the diagrams. Cut each strip set into 8 segments, 2½" wide, for a total of 24 segments from each unit.

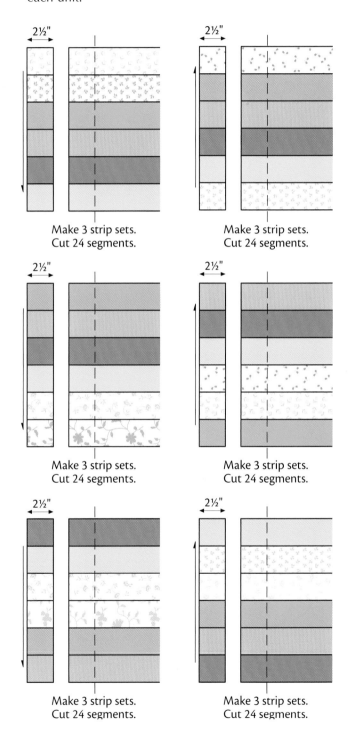

Make 3 strip sets.
Cut 24 segments.

Make 3 strip sets.
Cut 24 segments.

Make 3 strip sets.
Cut 24 segments.

Make 3 strip sets.
Cut 24 segments.

Make 3 strip sets.
Cut 24 segments.

Make 3 strip sets.
Cut 24 segments.

2. Combine segments 1–6 as shown to make a block. Make 24 blocks. Press the seam allowances in one direction in 12 blocks and in the opposite direction in 12 blocks. This will make it easier when joining blocks together.

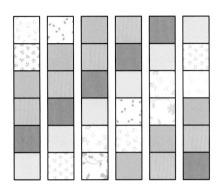

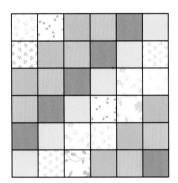

Make 24.

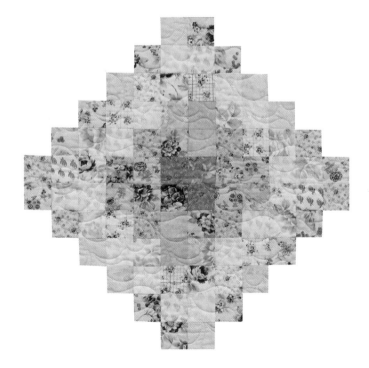

ASSEMBLING THE QUILT TOP

1. Arrange the blocks in six rows of four blocks each, rotating the blocks as shown.

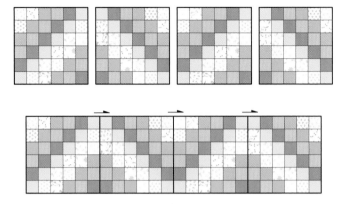

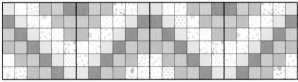

Make 6.

2. As you position the blocks, rotate rows 2, 4, and 6 as shown. Sew the rows together, pressing the seams in opposite directions from row to row.

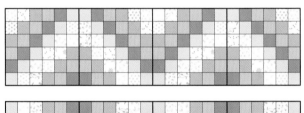

MAGIC CARPET

3. Join the rows and press the seam allowances in one direction.

4. Add the 1½"-wide inner-border strips, referring to "Adding Borders" on page 20.

5. Add the 6¼"-wide outer-border strips in the same manner.

FINISHING YOUR QUILT

1. Mark the quilt top with the design of your choice. Layer with batting and backing. Baste. Hand or machine quilt as desired.

2. Referring to "Binding the Edges" on page 25, cut 2¼"-wide bias strips for binding. Make a total of 306" of bias binding and sew it to the quilt.

3. Make and attach a label to the quilt.

By Nancy J. Martin, Kingston, Washington, 2007.
Quilted by Frankie Schmidt, Kenmore, Washington.

SUNNY Days

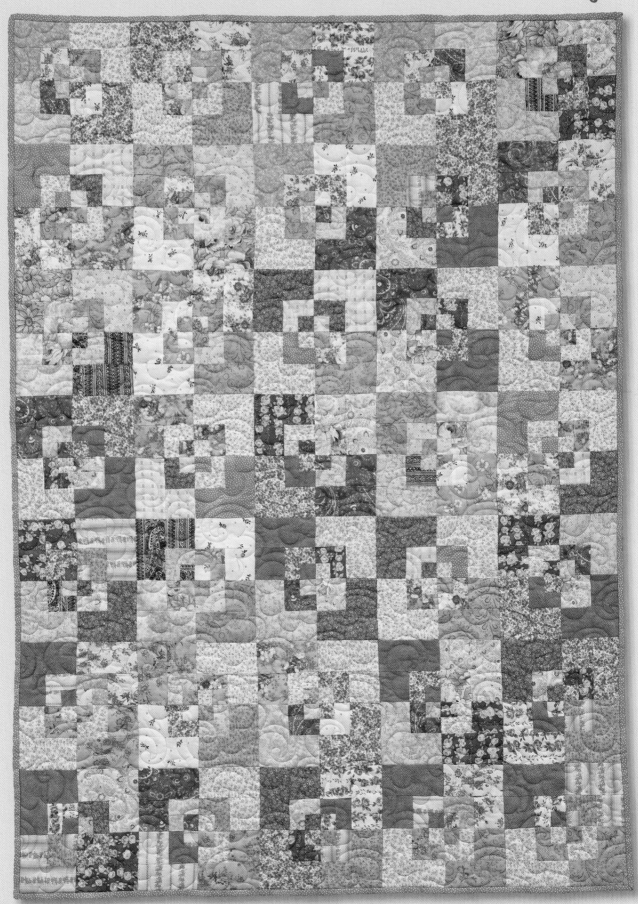

the fresh blue and yellow floral fabrics were the perfect choice for this quilt, which was inspired by a Judy Hopkins design, "Arctic Nights." Judy's version of this quilt is featured on the cover of her book Triangle-Free Quilts, which is filled with wonderful quilts. Judy's book is no longer in print, but it is available through Feathered Star Productions (www.marshamccloskey.com/judhopbook.html).

Finished Size: 40½" x 56½" — Block Size: 8" x 8"

MATERIALS

Note: This quilt does not use half strips.

24 strips, 2½" x 42", of yellow and light blue prints

24 strips, 2½" x 42", of darker blue prints

2¾ yards of fabric for backing

½ yard of fabric for bias binding

48" x 64" piece of batting

MAKING THE BLOCKS

1. Layer a 2½" x 42" light strip and a 2½" x 42" dark strip right sides together, aligning the long edges. Square up one end of this layered pair of strips and then cut:

    3 rectangles, 2½" x 4½" (A)

    3 squares, 2½" x 2½" (B)

    3 rectangles, 1½" x 2½" (C)

    Set these pieces aside.

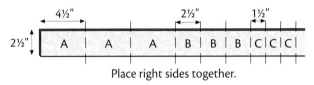

Place right sides together.

2. From the remaining length, trim the layered strips to 1½" by 11".

3. Sew the 1½" x 11" layered strips along the long edges to make a strip set. From this strip set, cut a total of six segments, 1½" wide.

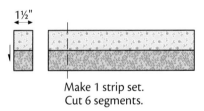

Make 1 strip set.
Cut 6 segments.

4. Join a strip-set segment from step 3 to each of the C rectangles from step 1 as shown, being careful to orient the strip-set segments in the correct direction for each combination. Make three of each combination. The units should measure 2½" x 2½" (raw edge to raw edge).

Make 3.   Make 3.

5. Join the B squares from step 1 to the units from step 4 as shown, being careful to add the correct light or dark square to the unit. Make three of each combination.

Make 3. Make 3.

6. Stitch the A rectangles from step 1 to the units from step 5 as shown, being careful to add the correct light or dark rectangle. Make three dark units and three light units. The units should measure 4½" x 4½".

Make 3. Make 3.

7. Repeat steps 1–6 with the remaining light and dark strips. When you have cut and stitched all 24 sets of strips, you will have 72 light units and 72 dark units.

8. Randomly mix and match two light and two dark units to make a block. Make 35 blocks as shown. You will have two light and two dark units left over. You may want to wait until all the blocks are arranged before pressing the final seam allowance. Once the blocks are arranged, you can press the seams so that they will butt together.

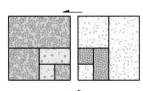

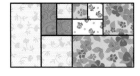

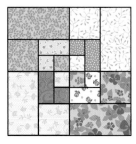

Make 35.

ASSEMBLING THE QUILT TOP

Arrange the blocks to make seven horizontal rows of five blocks each. Note that the blocks are arranged so that the darker blue fabrics appear at the upper left and lower right. Sew the blocks into rows. Press the seams in opposite directions from row to row. Sew the rows together. Press the seams in one direction.

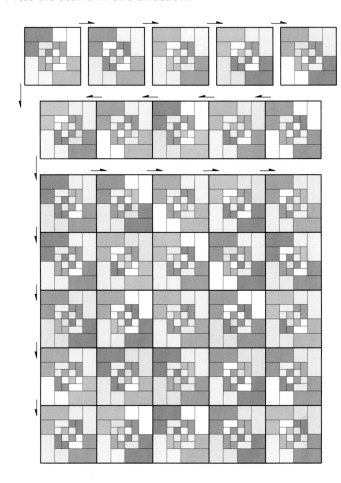

FINISHING YOUR QUILT

1. Mark the quilt top with the design of your choice. Layer with batting and backing. Baste. Hand or machine quilt as desired.

2. Referring to "Binding the Edges" on page 25, cut 2¼"-wide bias strips for binding. Make a total of 202" of bias binding.

3. Make and attach a label to the quilt.

By Nancy J. Martin, Kingston, Washington, 2007.
Quilted by Frankie Schmidt, Kenmore, Washington.

AROUND the Town

I used the Chelsea Boutique fabric collection, with polka dots and paisley prints, for the blocks in this quilt. The dark and light units alternate to make a simple 12" block. When set together, some of the blocks are rotated, forming a barn raising–type design. This quilt is proof that simple blocks can create a stunning design.

Finished Size: 60" x 60" — Block Size: 12" x 12"

MATERIALS

36 strips, 2½" x 22", of light prints

36 strips, 2½" x 22", of dark (teal, brown, and rose) prints

1⅞ yards of floral print for border and binding

3⅞ yards of fabric for backing

68" x 68" piece of batting

CUTTING

From *18* of the light strips, cut:
72 rectangles, 2½" x 4½"

From *18* of the dark strips, cut:
72 rectangles, 2½" x 4½"

From the floral print, cut from the lengthwise grain:
2 strips, 6¼" x 48½"

2 strips, 6¼" x 60"

MAKING THE BLOCKS

1. Stitch a light 2½"-wide strip to a dark 2½"-wide strip along the long edges to make a strip set. Press the seam allowances toward the dark strip. Make a total of 18 strip sets and cut into 144 segments, 2½" wide.

Make 18 strip sets.
Cut 144 segments.

2. Stitch a light and dark strip-set segment to each 2½" x 4½" light rectangle and dark rectangle as shown.

Make 72 of each.

3. Arrange five dark and four light units as shown and sew together to make a block. Make eight blocks. These will be referred to as dark blocks.

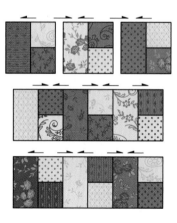

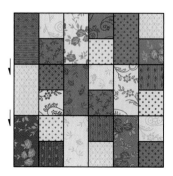

Make 8.

4. Arrange four dark and five light units as shown and sew together to make a block. Make eight blocks. These will be referred to as light blocks.

Make 8.

ASSEMBLING THE QUILT TOP

1. To create a barn raising–type design, arrange the light and dark blocks as shown below. There should be four dark blocks at the center of the quilt and one at each corner.

2. Sew the blocks into rows, pressing the seams in opposite directions from row to row. Sew the rows together.

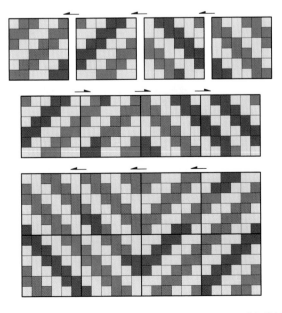

3. Add the 6¼"-wide border strips, referring to "Adding Borders" on page 20.

FINISHING YOUR QUILT

1. Mark the quilt top with the design of your choice. Layer with batting and backing. Baste. Hand or machine quilt as desired.

2. Referring to "Binding the Edges" on page 25, cut 2¼"-wide bias strips for binding. Make a total of 250" of bias binding.

3. Make and attach a label to the quilt.

By Nancy J. Martin, Kingston, Washington, 2007.
Quilted by Wanda Rains, Kingston, Washington.

POSY Pots

these whimsical appliquéd pots of flowers with their button centers make me smile each time I look at them. The blue and red diagonal chain designs end in a colorful patchwork border, resulting in a cheerful and nicely balanced combination of appliqué and patchwork.

Finished Size: 62½" x 62½" — Block Size: 10" x 10"

MATERIALS

9 strips, 2½" x 22", of blue print for pieced blocks

7 strips, 2½" x 22", of red print for pieced blocks

12 strips, 2½" x 22", of tan prints for flowerpots

10 strips, 2½" x 22", of green prints for leaves and stems

3 strips, 2½" x 22", *each* of assorted red and blue prints for flowers

45 strips, 2½" x 22", of assorted red, blue, green, tan, and light prints for border

2⅓ yards of white print for appliqué background and blocks

3¾ yards of fabric for backing

½ yard of fabric for bias binding

36 assorted buttons for flower centers*

70" x 70" piece of batting

Do not use buttons if a toddler will use the quilt.

CUTTING

From 9 of the blue print strips, cut:

65 squares, 2½" x 2½"

From 7 of the red print strips, cut:

52 squares, 2½" x 2½"

From the white print, cut:

12 squares, 11" x 11"

78 squares, 2½" x 2½"

26 rectangles, 2½" x 4½"

26 rectangles, 2½" x 6½"

MAKING THE APPLIQUÉ BLOCKS

Refer to "Paper-Patch Appliqué" on page 17, or use your preferred method to make the appliqué blocks.

1. Use the patterns on page 41 to make templates for appliqué pieces 1–5.

2. Stitch three 2½" x 22" tan strips together to make a pieced fabric for the flowerpots. Make four strip sets and cut 3 flowerpots (using Template 3) from each strip set for a total of 12.

Make 4 strip sets.
Cut 3 flowerpots from each set.

3. Trace template 4 and cut 19 red and 17 blue flowers. Trace and cut the stems and leaves, or make bias stems, referring to page 18.

4. Fold each 11" white background square in half vertically and horizontally to find the center point; crease lightly. Use these creases and the placement guide on page 42 to help you position the appliqués on the background squares.

5. Pin or baste the appliqué in place as shown. Using your preferred method, appliqué the stems, flowerpot, flowers, and leaves to the background fabric. Make 12 appliqué blocks, 7 of the red and 5 of the blue; then trim each to 10½" square.

Make 7.   Make 5.

MAKING THE CHAIN BLOCKS

Arrange five blue and four red 2½" squares with the white print squares and rectangles to make a block as shown. Sew the patches into rows. Sew the rows together to make a block. Make 13 blocks.

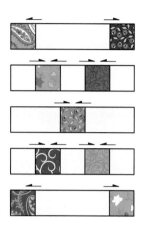

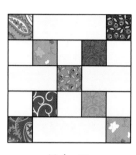

Make 13.

ASSEMBLING THE QUILT TOP

1. Arrange the pieced and appliquéd blocks in five horizontal rows of five blocks each, alternating them as shown. Odd-numbered rows begin with pieced blocks while even-numbered rows begin with appliqué blocks.

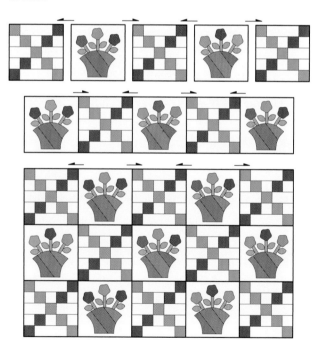

2. Sew the blocks into rows. Then join the rows.

3. Sew three of the assorted strips of different colors for the border together to make a strip set. Make 15 strip sets and cut them into a total of 112 segments, 2½" wide.

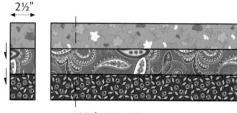

2½"

Make 15 strip sets.
Cut 112 segments.

4. Stitch 25 segments together for the top and bottom border strips. Sew a border strip to the top and bottom of the quilt.

5. Stitch 31 segments together for each of the side border strips. Sew a border strip to each side of the quilt.

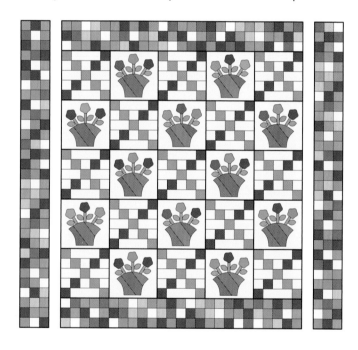

FINISHING YOUR QUILT

1. Mark the quilt top with the design of your choice. Layer with batting and backing. Baste. Hand or machine quilt as desired.

2. Referring to "Binding the Edges" on page 25, cut 2¼"-wide bias strips for binding. Make a total of 260" of bias binding.

3. Securely stitch a button in the center of each flower.

4. Make and attach a label to the quilt.

Patterns do not include seam allowances.

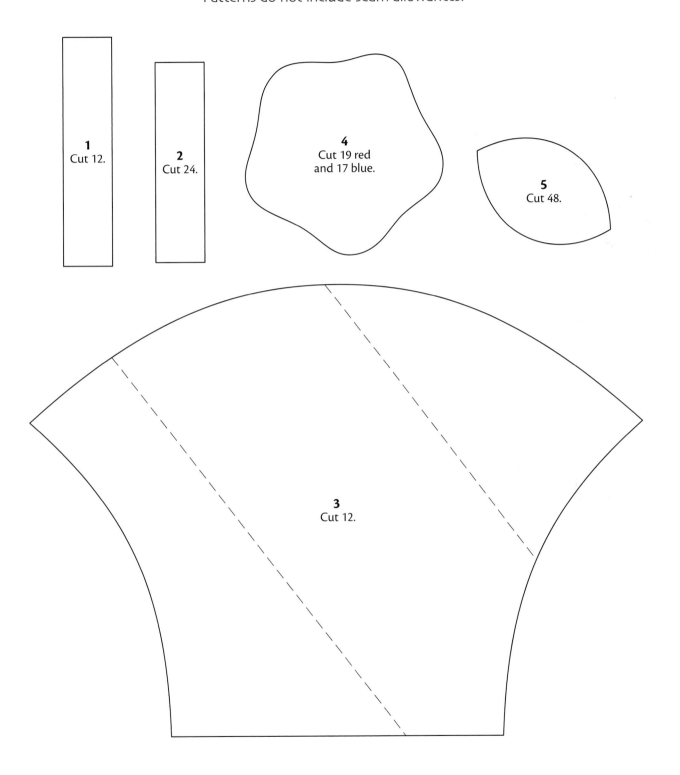

1
Cut 12.

2
Cut 24.

4
Cut 19 red
and 17 blue.

5
Cut 48.

3
Cut 12.

Placement guide

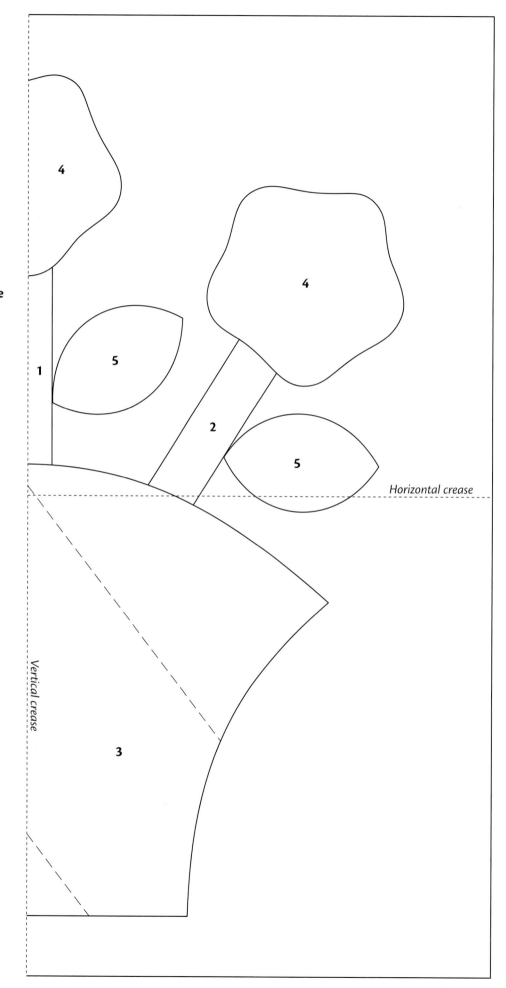

4

4

5

1

2

5

Horizontal crease

Vertical crease

3

By Cleo Nollette, Seattle, Washington, 2007.
Quilted by Shelly Nolte, Kingston, Washington.

STRING Square

this String Square design is a great choice when you need a quilt in a hurry. With strip piecing you can whip up the blocks in no time, and the wide borders let you finish quickly. Use one of your favorite print fabrics for the border and choose the other fabrics to coordinate with it.

Finished Size: 63¼" x 85⅞" — Block Size: 8" x 8"

MATERIALS

48 strips, 2½" x 22", in coordinating colors for blocks

½ yard *each* of 4 light prints for alternate blocks and setting triangles

2⅓ yards of floral print for outer border and binding

⅜ yard of dark print for inner border

5¼ yards of fabric for backing

72" x 94" piece of batting

CUTTING

From *each* of the 4 light prints, cut:*

4 squares, 9¼" x 9¼", for a total of 16 squares. Cut twice diagonally to make 64 triangles (4 are extra).

5 squares, 6⅝" x 6⅝", for a total of 20 squares. Cut squares diagonally in half to yield 40 triangles (4 are extra).

From the dark print for inner border, cut:

6 strips, 1½" x 42"

From the floral print, cut:

7 strips, 8¼" x 42"

*Be sure to keep the triangles cut from different-sized squares separate so that you will have the straight grain along the outer edges of the quilt. Label them if desired.

MAKING THE BLOCKS

1. Sew the 2½" x 22" strips into random sets of four strips each. Make 12 strip sets. Cut each set into 2 segments, 8½" wide, to make a total of 24 segments.

8½"

Make 12 strip sets.
Cut 24 segments.

2. Make 15 alternate blocks by stitching four triangles cut from the 9¼" squares together, using one of each light print.

Make 15.

3. Make 16 half blocks for the quilt edges by stitching two triangles cut from the 6⅝" squares together, using different light prints. Reserve four triangles for the quilt corners.

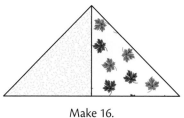

Make 16.

Reserve 4 for corners.

ASSEMBLING THE QUILT TOP

1. Arrange the blocks cut from strip sets (oriented in the same direction), alternate blocks, and half blocks in diagonal rows. Sew the blocks into rows and press toward the strip-pieced blocks.

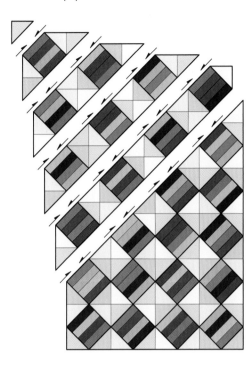

2. Join the rows to form the quilt top, adding the four reserved corner triangles.

3. Add the 1½"-wide inner-border strips, referring to "Adding Borders" on page 20.

4. Add the 8¼"-wide outer-border strips in the same manner.

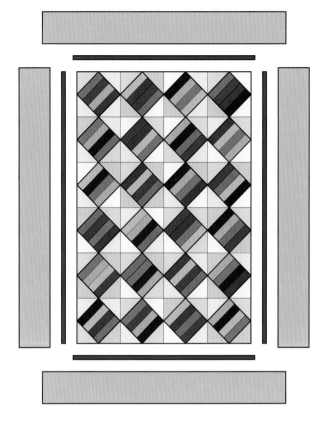

FINISHING YOUR QUILT

1. Mark the quilt top with the design of your choice. Layer with batting and backing. Baste. Hand or machine quilt as desired.

2. Referring to "Binding the Edges" on page 25, cut 2¼"-wide bias strips for binding. Make a total of 309" of bias binding.

3. Make and attach a label to the quilt.

By Cleo Nollette, Seattle, Washington, 2006.
Quilted by Frankie Schmidt, Kenmore, Washington.

STRIP Pinwheel

Vibrant colors *shout "springtime"*

in this lively collection of fabrics. The turquoise and

pink pinwheels keep your eye moving across this ener-

getic quilt. While you can make this quilt in any color

combination, it's the perfect opportunity to use fun,

bright prints or to try colors you might not normally

work with.

Finished Size: 57¼" x 72½"
Block Size: 15¼" x 15¼"

MATERIALS

48 strips, 2½" x 22", of coordinating colors and
    prints (pink, purple, green, turquoise) for blocks

⅞ yard of pink print for blocks

⅞ yard *total* of turquoise prints for blocks

⅓ yard of turquoise print for inner border

1 yard of turquoise print for outer border

3¾ yards of fabric for backing

⅝ yard of fabric for bias binding

66" x 81" piece of batting

CUTTING

From the pink print, cut:
12 squares, 8⅞" x 8⅞". Cut twice diagonally to
    make 48 triangles.

From the turquoise prints for blocks, cut:
12 squares, 8⅞" x 8⅞". Cut twice diagonally to
    make 48 triangles.

From the turquoise print for inner border, cut:
6 strips, 1½" x 42"

From the turquoise print for outer border, cut:
6 strips, 5" x 42"

MAKING THE BLOCKS

1. Stitch a pink triangle to a turquoise triangle as shown.
    Make 48 pairs, making sure that the color placement
    is identical in all pairs.

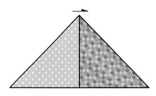

Make 48.

2. Sew the 2½" x 22" strips into random sets of four strips
    each. Make 12 strip sets. Press all seams in one
    direction.

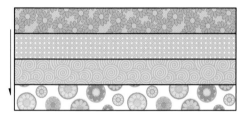

Make 12 strip sets.

3. Cut each strip set into two 8½" squares for a total
    of 24. Cut each square once diagonally to make 48
    triangles. Do all of the cutting with the strips right side
    up, making sure all the diagonal cuts are in the same
    direction.

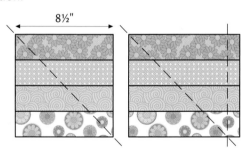

8½"

4. Assemble the triangle units from step 1 with the strip-
    pieced triangles to make a square unit.

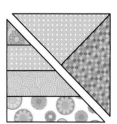 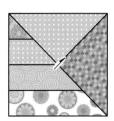

5. Assemble four of the square units to make a block. Make 12 blocks.

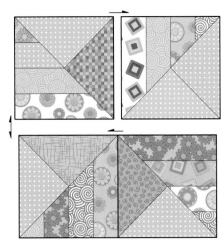

Make 12.

PRESS OPEN

To reduce bulk in the centers of the blocks, press the seams open.

ASSEMBLING THE QUILT TOP

1. Arrange the blocks into four rows of three blocks each. Sew the rows together, pressing the seams in opposite directions from row to row. Join the rows to make the quilt top. Press the seams in one direction.

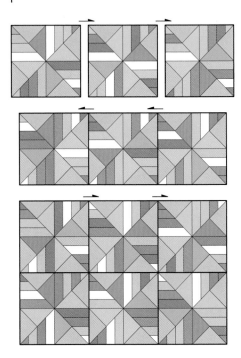

2. Add the 1½"-wide inner-border strips, referring to "Adding Borders" on page 20.

3. Add the 5"-wide outer-border strips in the same manner.

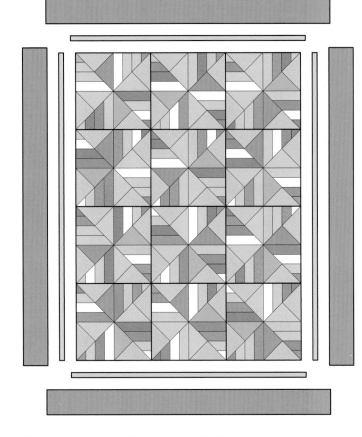

FINISHING YOUR QUILT

1. Mark the quilt top with the design of your choice. Layer with batting and backing. Baste. Hand or machine quilt as desired.

2. Referring to "Binding the Edges" on page 25, cut 2¼"-wide bias strips for binding. Make a total of 270" of bias binding.

3. Make and attach a label to the quilt.

By Nancy J. Martin, Kingston, Washington, 2007.
Quilted by Shelly Nolte, Kingston, Washington.

BOXING Day

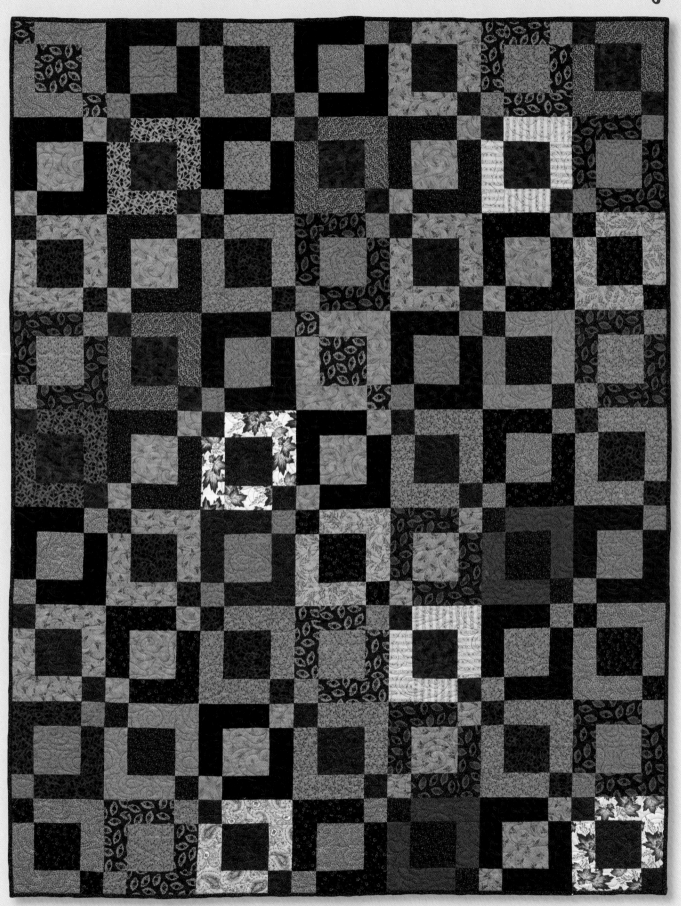

Boxing Day *is a great pattern to use up all of your leftover strips from other projects. This design reminds me of pretty little presents or boxes all wrapped up for a gift exchange. Each block uses just two fabrics—the light and dark versions of the block alternate to form a pleasing overall design.*

Finished Size: 56½" x 72½" — Block Size: 8" x 8"

MATERIALS

Your strips must be at least 22" long after squaring up the ends and removing selvages.

32 strips, 2½" x 22", of light prints

31 strips, 2½" x 22", of dark prints

1 fat quarter *each* of 4 light fabrics

1 fat quarter *each* of 4 dark fabrics

½ yard of dark print for bias binding

3⅞ yards of fabric for backing

65" x 81" piece of batting

CUTTING

From *each* of the 32 light strips and 31 dark strips, cut:

2 rectangles, 2½" x 6½" (64 light and 62 dark total)

2 rectangles, 2½" x 4½" (64 light and 62 dark total)

From *each* of the light and dark fat quarters, cut:

8 squares, 4½" x 4½" (64 total)

16 squares, 2½" x 2½" (128 total)

MAKING THE BLOCKS

You will make two color combinations of this block: blocks with light centers and dark edges, and blocks with dark centers and light edges. Pair up your fabrics, choosing one light and one dark for each block.

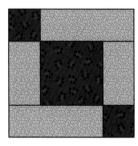

1. Stitch a light 2½" x 4½" rectangle to each side of a dark 4½" square.

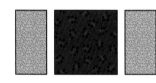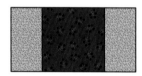

2. Stitch a dark 2½" square to a 2½" x 6½" light rectangle. Make two.

Make 2.

3. Join the units from step 2 to the top and bottom of the unit from step 1. Make sure the dark squares are in opposite diagonal corners. Make 32 blocks with dark centers and light strips on the outside edges.

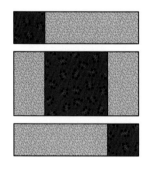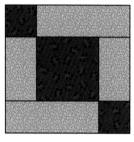

Make 32.

4. Reversing the colors, make 31 blocks with light centers and dark strips on the outside edges.

Make 31.

ASSEMBLING THE QUILT TOP

1. Arrange and sew the blocks into nine rows of seven blocks each, alternating the blocks with the light and dark outside edges. The four corners of the quilt should all have blocks with light outer edges. Press the seam allowances toward the blocks with dark outer edges.

2. Join the rows, matching seams. Press.

FINISHING YOUR QUILT

1. Mark the quilt top with the design of your choice. Layer with batting and backing. Baste. Hand or machine quilt as desired.

2. Referring to "Binding the Edges" on page 25, cut 2¼"-wide bias strips for binding. Make a total of 268" of bias binding.

3. Make and attach a label to the quilt.

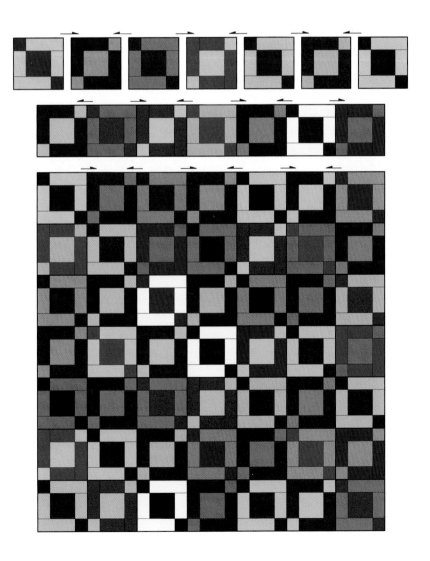

By Nancy J. Martin, Kingston, Washington, 2007.
Quilted by Wanda Rains, Kingston, Washington.

BARN Raising

Simple squares and triangles form a light and dark design area in each block. Rotating the blocks as you would do for a Log Cabin quilt creates bands of color that form this Barn Raising design. You can also set the blocks in many other ways, as you would typical Log Cabin blocks.

Finished Size: 52" x 72" — Block Size: 10" x 10"

MATERIALS

30 strips, 2½" x 22", of light prints for blocks

30 strips, 2½" x 22", of dark prints for blocks

14 strips, 2½" x 22", of accent print for blocks and inner border

⅓ yard *each* of 3 light fabrics for blocks

⅓ yard *each* of 3 dark fabrics for blocks

1 yard of medium print for outer border

3½ yards of fabric for backing

½ yard of fabric for binding

60" x 80" piece of batting

CUTTING

From *3* of the light strips, cut:
24 squares, 2½" x 2½"

From *3* of the dark strips, cut:
24 squares, 2½" x 2½"

From the accent strips, cut:
24 squares, 2½" x 2½"

11 strips, 1½" x 22"

From *each* of the 3 light fabrics, cut:
4 squares, 8" x 8" (12 total)

From *each* of the 3 dark fabrics, cut:
4 squares, 8" x 8" (12 total)

From the medium print, cut:
6 strips, 5¼" x 42"

MAKING THE BLOCKS

1. Using the 2½" x 22" light strips and following the illustrations below, sew three strip sets in each combination to make the units for the blocks. Cut each strip set into 8 segments, 2½" wide, for a total of 24 segments from each combination.

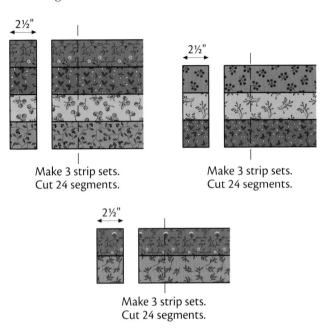

Make 3 strip sets.
Cut 24 segments.

Make 3 strip sets.
Cut 24 segments.

Make 3 strip sets.
Cut 24 segments.

2. Using the 2½" x 22" dark strips, repeat step 1. Cut each strip set into 8 segments, 2½" wide, for a total of 24 segments from each combination.

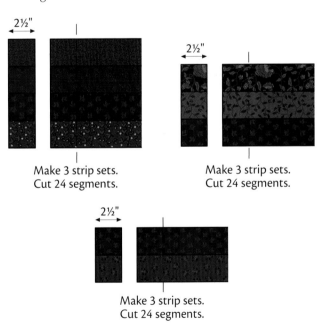

Make 3 strip sets.
Cut 24 segments.

Make 3 strip sets.
Cut 24 segments.

Make 3 strip sets.
Cut 24 segments.

3. Pair an 8" light square with an 8" dark square to make bias squares, referring to "Basic Bias-Square Technique" on page 14. Repeat with all the 8" squares. Cut four squares, 2½" x 2½" from each pieced unit, for a total of 96 bias squares.

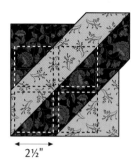

2½"

Cut 96.

4. Sew the light and dark units, bias squares, and accent squares into rows as shown. Stitch the rows together to make a block. Make 24 blocks.

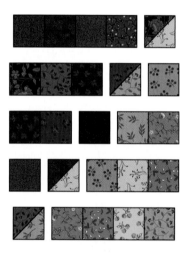

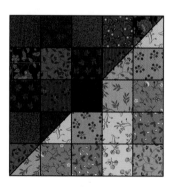

Make 24.

ASSEMBLING THE QUILT TOP

1. Arrange the blocks into six rows of four blocks each, rotating them as shown. Sew blocks together in rows, pressing in opposite directions from row to row. Join the rows to make the quilt top.

2. Join the 1½"-wide accent strips for the inner border strips. Add the inner-border strips, referring to "Adding Borders" on page 20.

3. Add the 5¼"-wide outer-border strips in the same manner.

FINISHING YOUR QUILT

1. Mark the quilt top with the design of your choice. Layer with batting and backing. Baste. Hand or machine quilt as desired.

2. Referring to "Binding the Edges" on page 25, cut 2¼"-wide bias strips for binding. Make a total of 258" of bias binding.

3. Make and attach a label to the quilt.

By Nancy J. Martin, Kingston, Washington, 2007.
Quilted by Wanda Rains, Kingston, Washington.

HOLLY Stars

Holly Stars, *with its appliquéd holly leaves, reflects the bright red and green colors of the Christmas season. The pieced units in each Star block are carefully arranged so the striped pieces alternate directions, eliminating tedious seam matching and bulky seams.*

Finished Size: 75" x 75" — Block Size: 30½"

MATERIALS

109 strips, 2½" x 22", of red prints for blocks and inner border*

32 strips, 2½" x 22", of green prints for blocks

1⅝ yards of green fabric for appliqué and outer border

4¾ yards of fabric for backing

⅝ yard of fabric for bias binding

83" x 83" piece of batting

*108 strips will be enough if you use leftover pieces from your strip sets for the pieced inner border.

CUTTING

From the green fabric, cut:
7 strips, 5¼" x 42"

MAKING THE BLOCK CENTERS

1. Sew 64 of the 2½" x 22" red strips into random sets of four strips each. Make 16 strip sets. Cut each strip set into two segments 8⅛" wide; cut a total of 32 segments.

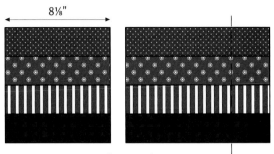

Make 16 strip sets.
Cut 32 segments.

2. Trim these segments to measure 8⅛" x 8⅛".

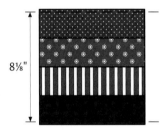

3. Sew four of these segments together to make the Star block center. Make four.

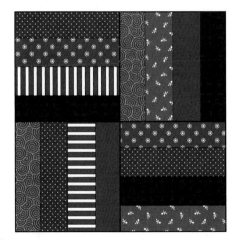

Make 4.

4. Referring to "Appliqué" on page 17, make a template using the pattern on page 61. Cut and prepare 20 holly pieces. Appliqué four holly leaves to the center of each Star block using the placement guide on page 61. Set the remaining holly leaves aside.

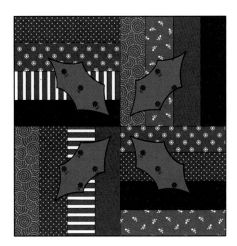

MAKING THE TRIANGLES

1. Sew 32 of the 2½" x 22" red strips together into random sets of four strips each. Press the seams all in one direction. Make eight strip sets. Cut each strip set into two segments 8½" wide to make a total of 16 segments. Repeat the process using the 32 green 2½" x 22" strips.

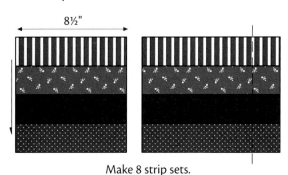

Make 8 strip sets.
Cut 16 segments.

Make 8 strip sets.
Cut 16 segments.

2. Cut each red segment in half diagonally to make 32 pieced triangles. Be sure to cut all of the red triangles in the direction shown.

Cut to make 32 triangles.

3. Cut each green segment in half diagonally to make 32 pieced triangles. Cut the green triangles in the opposite direction of the red as shown so that the seam allowances will butt together when aligned for piecing.

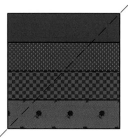

Cut to make 32 triangles.

4. Stitch the red triangles to the green triangles matching seams. Make 32 triangle units.

Make 32.

5. Stitch the appliquéd star centers, the remaining red units, and the triangle units together as shown to make a Star block. Be sure to orient the red units as shown to make assembly easy. Make four Star blocks.

Make 4.

ASSEMBLING THE QUILT TOP

1. Arrange the four Star blocks together as shown. In each block, make a diagonal crease in the corner that will be in the center of the quilt. Appliqué a holly leaf in the marked corner of each block using the placement guide on page 61.

 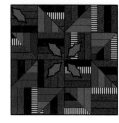

2. Sew the blocks into rows. Then join the rows.

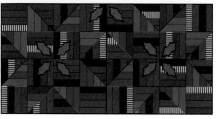

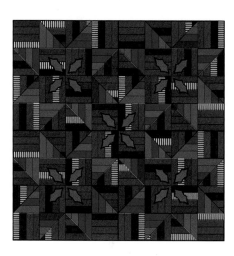

3. Stitch the remaining red 2½"-wide strips together for the inner border. Add the inner-border strips, referring to "Adding Borders" on page 20.

4. Add the 5¼"-wide outer-border strips in the same manner.

FINISHING YOUR QUILT

1. Mark the quilt top with the design of your choice. Layer with batting and backing; baste. Hand or machine quilt as desired.

2. Referring to "Binding the Edges" on page 25, cut 2¼"-wide bias strips for binding. Make a total of 310" of bias binding.

3. Make and attach a label to the quilt.

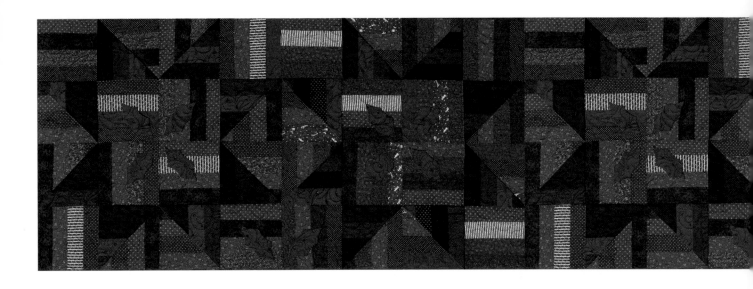

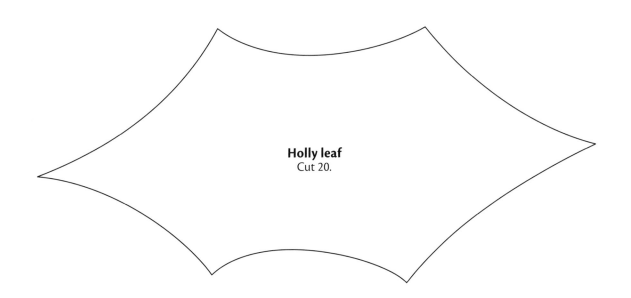

Holly leaf
Cut 20.

HOLLY STARS

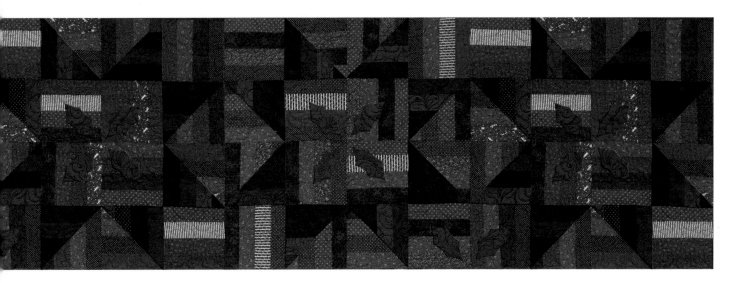

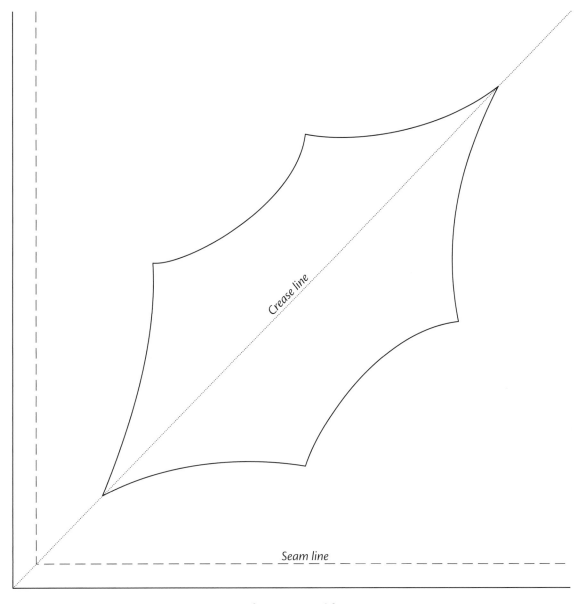

Crease line

Seam line

Placement guide

By Nancy J. Martin, Kingston, Washington, 2007.
Quilted by Frankie Schmidt, Kenmore, Washington.

FORTIES Four Patch

I love 1930s and '40s reproduction fabrics and this Four Patch block is a great way to showcase my collection. The block is made in two color combinations, reversing the light and dark fabrics, which creates the chain pattern that dances across the quilt.

Finished Size: 60½" x 76½" — Block Size: 8" x 8"

MATERIALS

8 strips, 2½" x 22", of red prints

8 strips, 2½" x 22", of blue prints

8 strips, 2½" x 22", of lavender prints

24 strips, 2½" x 22", of assorted tone-on-tone white prints

2 fat quarters *each* of red, blue, and lavender prints

4 fat quarters of tone-on-tone white prints

½ yard of tone-on-tone white print for inner border

1 yard of red print for outer border

3⅞ yards of fabric for backing

⅝ yard of blue print for bias binding

69" x 85" piece of batting

CUTTING

From *each* of the red, blue, and lavender fat quarters, cut:
8 squares, 4½" x 4½" (48 total, 16 of each color)

From *each* of the 4 tone-on-tone white fat quarters, cut:
12 squares, 4½" x 4½" (48 total)

From the white print for inner border, cut:
6 strips, 2½" x 42"

From the red print for outer border, cut:
7 strips, 4½" x 42"

MAKING THE BLOCKS

You will make two color combinations of this block, one with white 4½" squares and one with random pairings of red, blue, and lavender 4½" squares.

1. Make the four-patch units by stitching each 2½" x 22" white strip to a red, blue, or lavender strip to make 24 strip sets. Press the seam allowances toward the colored strips.

Make 24 strip sets.

2. Layer two sets of strips right sides together, having the dark and light strips facing each other as shown. Cut each layered pair of strip sets into eight segments, 2½" wide.

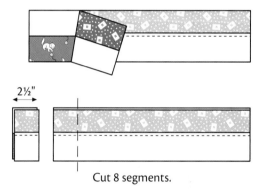

Cut 8 segments.

3. Stitch the segments together to make 96 four-patch units.

Make 96.

4. Combine two four-patch units with two colored 4½" squares to make 24 dark blocks.

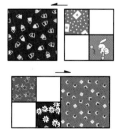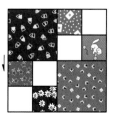

Make 24.

5. Combine two four-patch units with two white 4½"
   squares to make 24 light blocks.

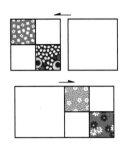 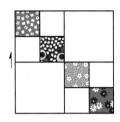

Make 24.

ASSEMBLING THE QUILT TOP

1. Arrange and sew the blocks into eight rows of six
   blocks each, alternating the dark and light blocks as
   shown. Press the seams in opposite directions from
   row to row. Sew the rows together and press.

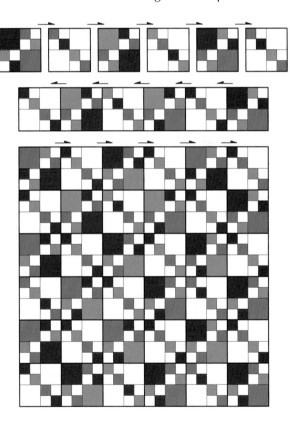

2. Referring to "Adding Borders" on page 20, add the
   2½"-wide inner-border strips.

3. Add the 4½"-wide outer-border strips in the same
   manner.

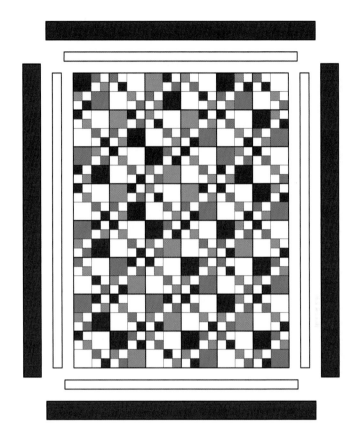

FINISHING YOUR QUILT

1. Mark the quilt top with the design of your choice.
   Layer with batting and backing. Baste. Hand or
   machine quilt as desired.

2. Referring to "Binding the Edges" on page 25, cut
   2¼"-wide bias strips for binding. Make a total of 282"
   of bias binding.

3. Make and attach a label to the quilt.

By Nancy J. Martin, Kingston, Washington, 2007.

TOTE Bag

travel in style with this classic tote bag sewn in a springtime color scheme. The roomy interior and sturdy handles are perfect to hold clothes or quilting items for a weekend trip.

Finished Size: 19" x 8½" x 9"

MATERIALS

6 strips, 2½" x 42", of assorted colors for handles

27 strips, 2½" x 22", of assorted colors for tote

1 yard of fabric for lining

36" x 40" piece of batting

2 yards of purchased piping

20" sport zipper

MAKING THE QUILTED FABRIC

1. Cut two pieces of batting and lining, each 22" x 18". These pieces are cut larger than necessary and will be trimmed later to the proper size.

2. Place the lining, right side down, then layer the batting on top of the lining. Using the 2½" x 22" strips, position the first strip in the middle of the batting. Place another strip on top of the first, right sides together and with raw edges even. Stitch through all the layers using a ¼" seam. Flip the strip over to the right side and press.

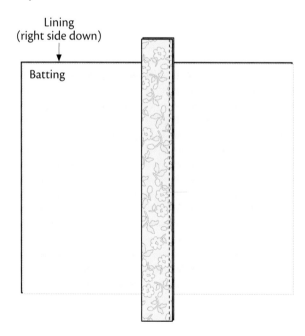

3. Layer the next strip on top of the one just pressed, right sides together and with raw edges even. Stitch with a ¼" seam. Continue stitching and flipping until you reach the edge of the batting.

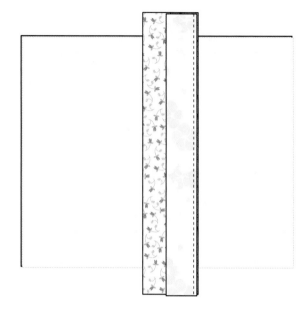

4. Turn the batting around and stitch and flip strips to cover the rest of the batting. Repeat the process to cover the second piece of batting and lining.

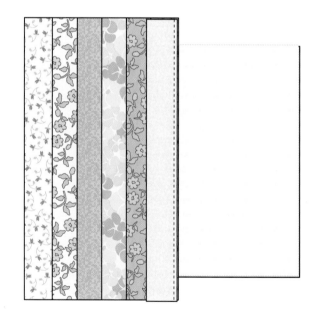

5. Trim each strip-quilted piece to measure 20" x 16½".

6. Cut two pieces of batting and two pieces of lining using the tote end pattern found on page 70. Use the same procedure to cover the batting and lining, beginning at the bottom on each tote end piece. Trim away the excess on the end of each strip so that it is even with the batting and lining.

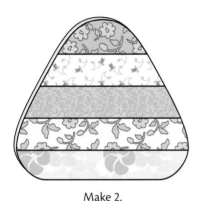

Make 2.

STITCHING THE TOTE

1. Add the zipper, following the directions in "Inserting a Zipper" on page 69. Overcast the long edges with an overcast or zigzag stitch on your machine. This will keep the fabric edges from fraying.

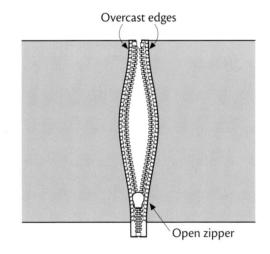

Overcast edges

Open zipper

2. Close the zipper and topstitch close to the folded edges on the right side of the fabric.

3. Stitch three 2½" x 42" strips together along the long edges for each tote handle. Press the seams open. Cut each strip to 34" long and 5½" wide. Cut two pieces of batting, 2¾" x 34".

4. Fold the handle in half lengthwise, right sides together. Place the handle fabric on top of the batting, and stitch ¼" from the raw edge, leaving one short end open. Turn right side out and press. Repeat for the remaining handle.

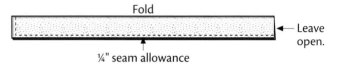

Fold

Leave open.

¼" seam allowance

5. Topstitch nine lines along the length of each handle, placing lines about ¼" apart.

6. Fold under the open end of the handle. Pin the handle ends on each side of the tote, 3" below the zipper and 3" from each end of the tote.

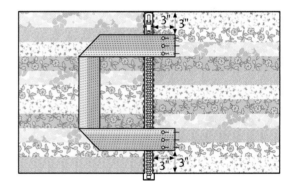

7. Machine stitch the ends of the handle to the tote as shown. Repeat steps 6 and 7 for the second handle.

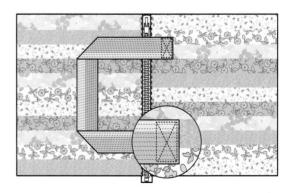

8. With right sides together, stitch the tote bag together along the bottom edge, using a ½"-wide seam allowance. Press the seam open.

9. To make the pull tab at the end of the zipper, cut a 2" x 4" piece of fabric from the lining fabric or other scraps. Fold in half crosswise with right sides together, and stitch along two sides using a ¼" seam allowance; leave the remaining side open. Clip the corners and turn right side out. Baste the tab to the end of the closed zipper that does not have the zipper pull, aligning the raw edges.

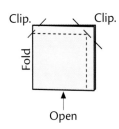

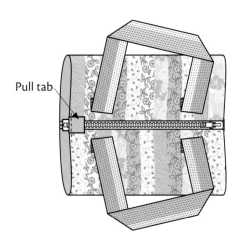

Baste pull tab in place.

FINISHING THE TOTE

1. Beginning in the middle of the bottom edge of each tote end, place the piping on the right side of the fabric with the raw edges even. Pin around the outside edge. Clip the piping seam allowance at the corner curves.

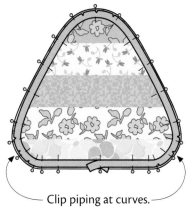

Clip piping at curves.

2. To create a smooth seam where the piping meets, trim the ends of the piping, leaving a ½" overlap. Pull both ends of the cord out of the fabric casing and trim ½" off each end of the cord. Overlap the ends of the piping as shown to create a smooth, even band of piping when pieces are joined. Stitch the piping in place using a zipper foot or cording foot.

3. With right sides together, pin the tote end to the tote and stitch together using a zipper foot or cording foot. Stitch with the tote end on top, and you will be able to stitch just inside the previous stitching line used for the piping. Remove the pins as you come to them; do not stitch over them. When stitching across the upper edge, stitch slowly as you near the zipper. Do not stitch through the zipper; stop and backstitch on either side of the zipper.

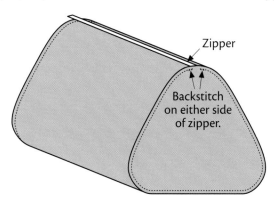

4. Open the zipper partially and stitch the remaining tote end to the tote in the same manner. Turn tote right sid out.

5. Cut a piece of cardboard to measure 8½" x 19". Cut two pieces of fabric, 9" x 20". With right sides together, stitch ¼" from the edge on three sides. Clip corners and turn to the right side. Insert cardboard inside and slip-stitch the open edge closed.

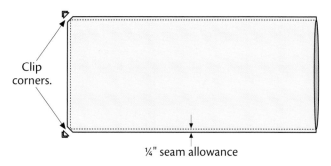

6. Place the fabric-covered cardboard in the bottom of the tote.

INSERTING A ZIPPER

1. Open the zipper and place it face down on the right side of the strip-quilted fabric, aligning the raw edges of the fabric and the edge of the zipper.

2. Using a zipper foot, stitch through all layers ¼" from the zipper teeth.

3. As you near the zipper pull, stop stitching and close the zipper. Continue stitching to the end.

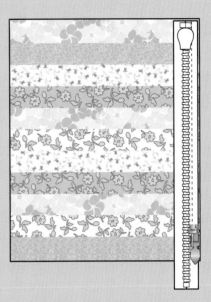

4. Repeat for the other side of the zipper on the remaining strip-quilted piece of fabric.

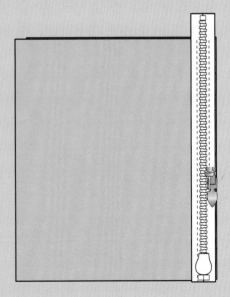

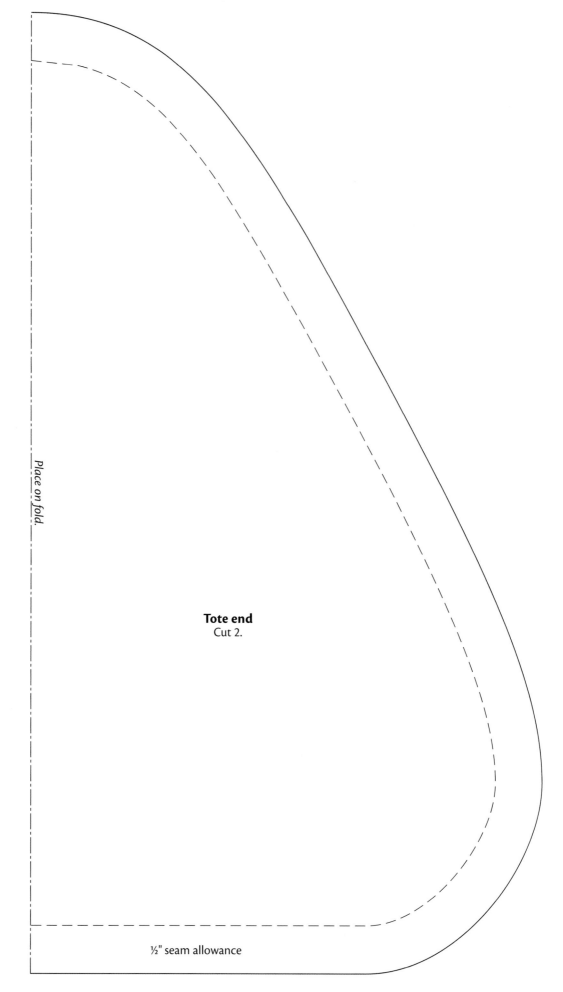

Place on fold.

Tote end
Cut 2.

½" seam allowance

By Nancy J. Martin, Kingston, Washington, 2006.

BOUDOIR pillow

this dainty little boudoir pillow with ruffled edges

will brighten up a favorite chair or add charm to a grouping of pillows

on a bed or sofa. The pillow shown coordinates with the quilt "Magic

Carpet" on page 28, but you can purchase extra fabric and make it

to coordinate with any of the quilts in the book. It has a lapped back

opening and is sized to fit a 12" x 16" pillow form.

Finished Size: 12" x 16", not including ruffle

MATERIALS

6 strips, 2½" x 22", of assorted colors

⅝ yard of floral print for ruffle and pillow back

12" x 16" pillow form

CUTTING

See the cutting diagram below for the most efficient use of the floral print.

From *each* of the 6 strips, cut:

2 strips, 2½" x 11" (12 total)

From the floral print, cut:

2 strips, 5" x 22"

2 pieces, 12" x 12½"

2 strips, 2" x 12½"

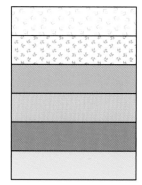

Floral print cutting diagram

MAKING THE PILLOW

1. Sew six 2½" x 11" strips together to form a strip set. Make two strip sets, varying the placement of the fabrics.

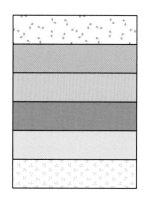

2. Crosscut each strip set into four segments, 2½" wide.

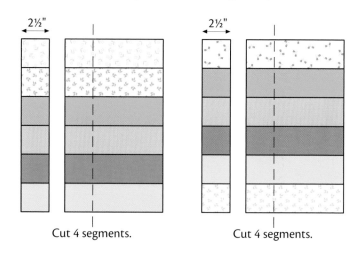

3. Stitch the segments together, varying the top and bottom fabric placement.

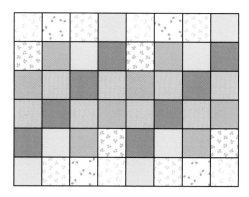

4. Fold a 5" x 22" strip of fabric right sides together for the ruffle. Stitch both short ends of the ruffle together with a ¼" seam. Clip corners. Repeat with the other 5" x 22" piece of fabric to make the second ruffle.

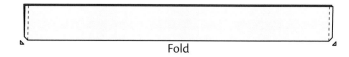

Fold

5. Turn the ruffles to the right side and sew a gathering stitch ¼" from the raw edges of each. Gather to 12½" long, the length of the sides of the pillow top.

6. Pin the gathered ruffles to each side of the pillow front, right sides together and with raw edges even. Ease fullness so the ruffle is evenly gathered. Baste the ruffles in place and remove the pins.

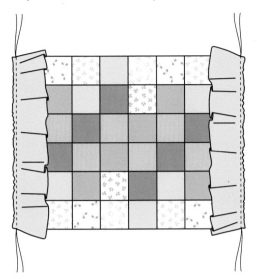

7. Fold the 2" x 12½" strips in half lengthwise, wrong sides together. Pin strips to each side of the pillow back, aligning the raw edges. Stitch each strip to the pillow back using a ¼" seam. Press flat.

Sew.

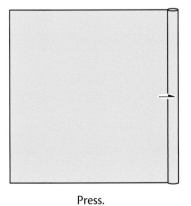

Press.

8. Overlap the pillow backs on top of the pillow front, right sides together, as shown. Pin.

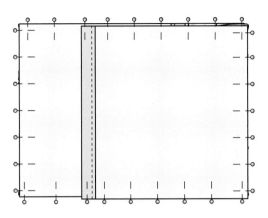

9. Stitch using a ⅜"-wide seam allowance. Clip the corners and turn right side out. Insert the pillow form through the opening. (Using a ⅜"-wide seam allowance allows the pillow cover to fit over the form tightly.)

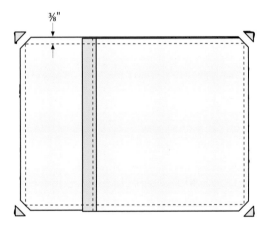

AUTUMN LEAVES Table Runner

By Cleo Nollette, Seattle, Washington, 2007.
Quilted by Frankie Schmidt, Kenmore, Washington.

Autumn leaves flutter in many directions on this pretty fall table runner. These 10 simple-to-stitch blocks can be sewn in no time and stitched into this unique table runner. You'll have plenty of time to whip up a hearty fall meal and set a charming, seasonal table.

Finished Size: 19" x 57" — Block Size: 6" x 6"

MATERIALS

23 strips, 2½" x 22", of light prints

9 strips, 2½" x 22", of dark prints

1 fat quarter of dark print for bias stems

¾ yard of leaf print for setting pieces

2 yards of fabric for backing

½ yard of fabric for bias binding

27" x 69" piece of batting

⅜" bias press bar

CUTTING

From the light strips, cut:
6 strips, 2½" x 14½"

5 rectangles, 2½" x 6½"

60 squares, 2½" x 2½"

From the dark strips, cut:
30 rectangles, 2½" x 4½"

10 squares, 2½" x 2½"

From the dark fat quarter, cut:
1⅛"-wide bias strips to total 40"

From the leaf print, cut:
8 triangles using template 1

2 triangles using template 2

1 rectangle, 10¼" x 20"

MAKING THE BLOCKS

1. Place a 2½" light square on top of a 2½" x 4½" dark rectangle, right sides together. Draw a line from corner to corner on the wrong side of the square. Stitch along the drawn line, then align the ¼" marking of your ruler with the stitching, and trim away the excess fabric. Press seams toward the dark fabric. Repeat to make 20 of these units.

Make 20.

2. Repeat step 1, drawing the diagonal line in the opposite direction. Make 10 units.

Make 10.

3. Place a light and a dark 2½" square right sides together. Draw a line from corner to corner on the wrong side of the light square. Stitch along the drawn line and then trim as before. Press the seam toward the dark fabric. Make 10 units.

Make 10.

4. Referring to "Bias Stems" on page 18, make bias tubes using the ⅜" bias press bar and the bias strips. Cut into approximately 10 lengths of 3⅝" and appliqué a stem by hand or machine to each of 10 light 2½" squares.

5. Arrange the units from steps 1–4 and the remaining light squares as shown to form a leaf block. Sew the units together. Make 10 blocks.

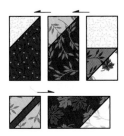

Make 10.

ASSEMBLING THE TABLE RUNNER

1. Stitch two leaf blocks to a light 2½" x 6½" rectangle, rotating the direction of each leaf. Make five units, changing the orientation of the leaves in each.

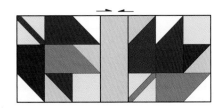

Make 5.

2. Stitch a 2½" x 14½" light strip to the left side of each set of leaf blocks.

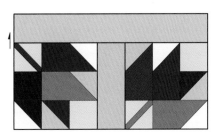

Make 5.

3. Add a 2½" x 14½" light strip to the right side of one set of leaf blocks.

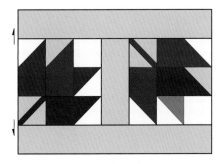

Make 1.

4. Stitch a leaf-print triangle cut from template 2 to opposite sides of the leaf block unit made in step 3. The triangles are cut oversize and will be trimmed later.

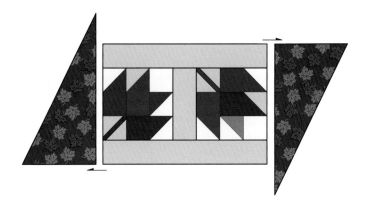

5. Stitch a leaf-print triangle cut from template 1 to each side of the remaining leaf block units.

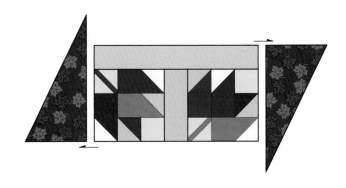

6. Cut the 10¼" x 20" leaf-print rectangle in half as shown, with the right side up.

7. Join the leaf block units and add a triangle cut in step 6 to each end of the table runner. Press.

8. Trim and square up the table runner as shown. Allow 1⅜" beyond the block points on the left side and 1⅜" beyond the sashing points on the right side. Also allow 1⅜" beyond the sashing points on the top and bottom. The blocks will appear to "float" against the background.

FINISHING THE TABLE RUNNER

1. Mark the table runner with the design of your choice. Layer with batting and backing. Baste. Hand or machine quilt as desired.

2. Referring to "Binding the Edges" on page 25, cut 2¼"-wide bias strips for binding. Make a total of 164" of bias binding.

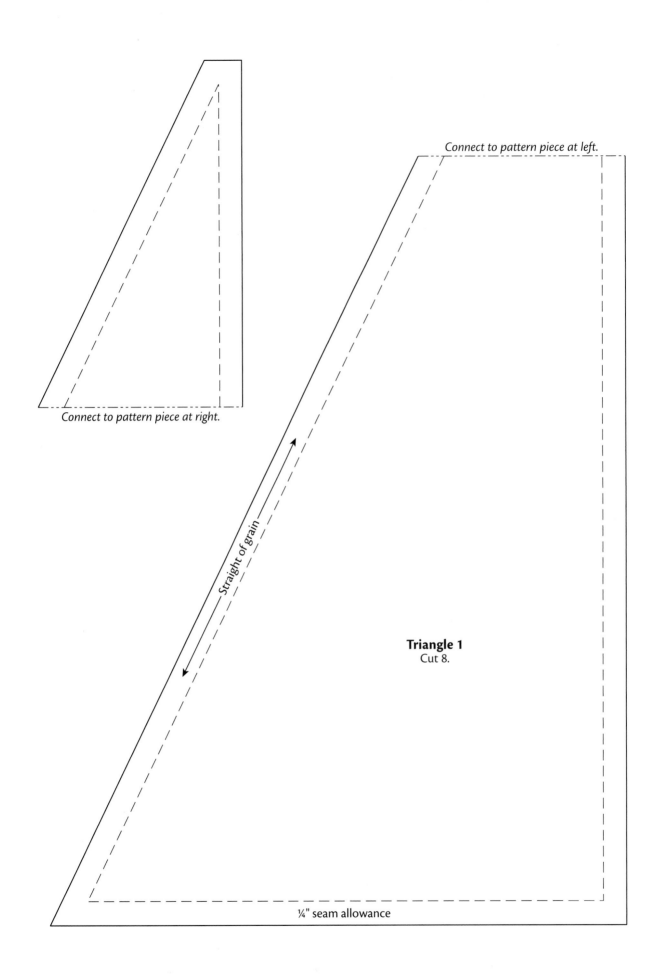

Connect to pattern piece at right.

Connect to pattern piece at left.

Straight of grain

Triangle 1
Cut 8.

¼" seam allowance

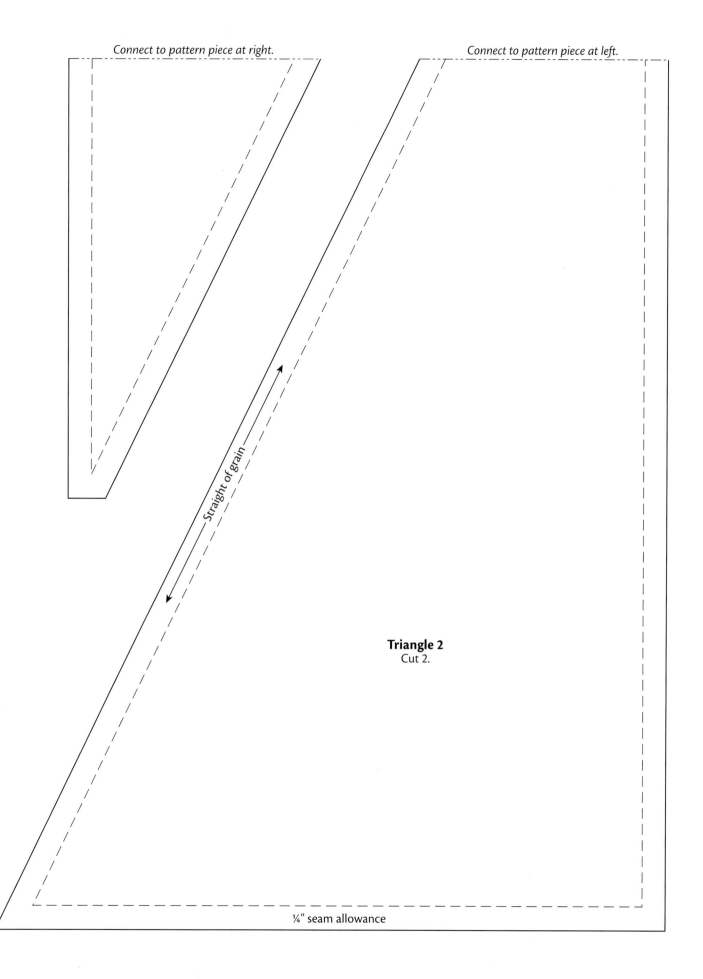

Connect to pattern piece at right.

Connect to pattern piece at left.

Straight of grain

Triangle 2
Cut 2.

¼" seam allowance

ABOUT the Author

-Nancy J. Martin is a talented teacher and quiltmaker who has written more than 45 books on quiltmaking. An innovator in the quilting industry, she introduced the Bias Square cutting ruler to eager quilters. Nancy was the 2002 recipient of the prestigious Silver Star Award. This recognition comes from Quilts, Inc., sponsor of the largest trade shows in the quilting industry, International Quilt Market and Festival. The award is presented annually to an individual whose artistry, enthusiasm, and promotion of quilting has made a lasting impact on the quilting industry as well as quilters everywhere.

Nancy and her husband, Dan, founded Martingale & Company, the publisher of America's Best-Loved Quilt Books®, in 1976. After 31 years of leadership at Martingale, the Martins sold the publishing company to their employees in 2007. They remain on the Board of Directors at Martingale, while enjoying more time for local activities in their hometown on the western shores of Puget Sound.